FRANK

by the same author

POETRY
Nervous Arcs
Botany Bay Document
The Hanging of Jean Lee
My Secret Life (chapbook)
The Fall
Vertigo: a Cantata
the sonnet according to 'm'
The Book of Ethel
kindness (artist's book)
XIII Poems
Jack & Mollie (& Her)
Euclid's Dog: 100 Algorithmic Poems
Warlines
The Cyprus Poems (chapbook)
element: the atomic weight & radius of love
Fifteeners
book (artist's book)

ANTHOLOGIES (EDITOR)
The Weekly Poem: 52 Exercises in Closed & Open Forms
Prayers of a Secular World (co-ed)

CHILDREN'S POETRY
Sukie's Suitcase
Barkwoofggrrr!
Esmé d'Arc Adds Up to More Than Zero

FRANK
Jordie Albiston

CELEBRATING

NATIONAL LIBRARY
OF AUSTRALIA
PUBLISHING

50 YEARS

Published by National Library of Australia Publishing
Canberra   ACT   2600

ISBN: 9781922507433

Publisher: Lauren Smith
Managing editor: Amelia Hartney
Designer: Andy Szikla
Image coordinator: Jemma Posch
Printed in China by C & C Offset Printing Co. Ltd
Printed on FSC®-certified paper.

FSC
www.fsc.org
MIX
Paper | Supporting
responsible forestry
FSC® C008047

Find out more about NLA Publishing: nla.gov.au/national-library-
publishing.

A catalogue record for this
book is available from the
National Library of Australia

for Andy

Out of whose wombe came the yce ?
and the hoary frost of heauen, who hath gendred it ?
The waters are hid as with a stone,
and the face of the deepe is frozen.

—Job 38: 29-30

Only those who have experienced it can fully appreciate what it means to be
without the sun day after day and week after week. Few men unaccustomed
to it can fight off its effects altogether, and it has driven some men mad.

—Alfred Lansing

Hauling, toiling, tireless on we tramp,
O'er vast plateau, sastrugi high,
O'er deep crevasse & ramp.
Hauling, toiling through blizzard and gale,
If it has to be done, then make of it fun,
For we're men of the Southern TRAIL.

—Frank Hurley

contents

§

§

THE MAWSON EXPEDITION

November 1912–January 1913

10 November 1912

after numerous attempts to push forward sledging section of Expedition we at last make a start blizzard breaking up & time getting short all anxious to get under weigh Robert Bage command Eric Webb magnetician & self general handy man & photographic arriving at "Five Mile" Depot total weight of equipment— Norwegian sledge-decking cooker & instrument boxes 74lbs/ Instruments primus & misc gear 184lbs/ Tent & legs 26lbs/ 3 sleeping-bags 31½lbs/ Clothes-boots 72lbs/ 5 Tins kerosene 50lbs/ Perks 14½lbs/ 7 Weeks food 350lbs = TOTAL 802½lbs meet Mawson Mertz Ninnis with dogs I take Cine film also snaps of party & following hearty hand shake & good wishes both sides bid fare-well after "Five Mile" our way lies up a steep slope & not being in good NICK our muscles feel the strain fall through many crevasses to our waists but no serious mishaps & then supports at "Eleven Mile" Depot 1130PM & good HOOSH & sleeping-bags DEAD tired

14 November 1912

mid-night (13th) *terrific conditions* wind blows up 70 miles per hour *terrific conditions* although our tent pitched in lee of supporting partys we have grave apprehensions of it whirling away in these "Gentle Zephyrs" ET now 9PM & wind bellowing 80 miles per hour seething drift pelts like sand blast fatal to have thin calico walls ripped by *terrific conditions* & seems impossible they can hold out much longer get out of bags 330PM nearly two hours to put on frozen garments like putting one's legs into stove pipes & all get frostbit if one gets cold in *terrific conditions* it is a job to warm up & much calorific value of food wasted however "it might always be worse"

16 November 1912

what a stagnant silence!   our ears so accustomed to continuous din—
ache   what a striking contrast to the blizzard's eternal roar   what a
place of excesses   our ears so accustomed to continuous din—   ache
Bob has ordered supports to throw snow onto tent to make some noise
what a place of excesses   every-sound-seems-frozen   Bob has ordered
supports to make some noise so we can go to sleep   our tent limp for
not the gentlest Zephyr stirs   every-sound-seems-frozen   what is going
to happen   our tent limp & not the gentlest Zephyr stirs   what a
contrast to the blizzard roar   what is going to happen   what a stagnant
silence!

17 November 1912

wondering what the folks at home are doing whilst we tramp this Great
Desolation   this morning hauling in very light drift but Sun & distance
hid by dense hazy cloud   light so diffused impossible to discriminate rise
from hollow   light casting no shadows the entire surface looking even &
blank   wondering what folks at home are doing   many falls over un-
seen obstacles but cover 5½ miles bringing total to 39 miles & one week
gone   at this point notice two tins kerosene missing a most serious
matter   Murphy & Laseron re-trace trail & find them 2½ miles astern
I-am-won-der-ing-what-folks-are-do-ing-at-home   plateau surface here
much torn & covered with large sastrugi an eloquent testimony of harsh
wind but a fine Sun-set this evening I secure several photographs
wondering what folks at home are doing whilst we tramp this Great
Desolation

19 November 1912

fortune is with us   weather delightfully calm & Sunshiny   surface good
as far as eye reach we are girdled by vast even plain   s-m-o-o-t-h
monotonous   devoid of any feature or mark at noon the Sun blazes
down we divest ourselves of all apparel & haul in singlets & underpants a
humorous sight in this un-dress regalia (extremely pleased none of Fair
Sex! among party)   how strange it seems with 60 miles of snow & ice
between Hut & us yet one feels heat as much as any Aust summer &
could easily partake in ice creams   I take snaps   turn in dog tired
1015PM

21 November 1912

how time flies!   twelve months ago we were just leaving Sydney—   a
skua gull visits to-day   try to snare him by baiting fishing line with piece
of pemmican he isn't having any   we have decided to lay Depot at this
camp 67½ miles from Hut   as I write in sleeping-bag I look out across
great snow field eleven miles to Northern horizon the Sun sinking in a
halo of gorgeous clouds has just dipped below & the sky a-glow with
prismatic flushings it will rise on the morrow without punctuation
spend afternoon assembling large snow mound 10 feet high & 12 in
diameter   in its centre we fit special flag vane 20 feet high   these two
marks to enable vision of Depot from 8 miles radius   Bob's eyes very
painful now the snow glare like ground glass I am just going to pop into
them ophthalmic tabaloids before turning in   how time flies!   twelve
months ago to-day we were just leaving Sydney—   hope to be off to-
morrow

22 November 1912

stay all day at 67½ mile camp which we christen "Southern Cross Depot" assist in Magnetic Observation & write up meteorological log supporting party leaves 630PM soon out of sight in low scudding drift it feels quite lonely bidding good-bye with last tie to civilization nevertheless sledging has its humour for in sorting our chattels to cut down every ounce of weight we find lid off Horlick's milk tin the "Perk bag" (containing delicacies) mixed with powdered milk & snow & Sun has thawed mixture & done the rest almonds raisins all a conglomerate mass & everything in a state of stickphast & refuses to leave bag (without ado we cut bag open & partake of mixture with relish)

24 November 1912

so disgusted with weather that I force my-self to make entry— a fort-night since we have seen any object other than SNOW— even that must be observed through goggles— leave Southern Cross in 35 mile wind— drift-cuts-the-face-&-wind-splits-the-lips— after long up-hill struggle against terrible wind— sledge frequently over-turned but still we plod— all we know to just keep it moving so terrific the turmoil & tumult around— wind after increase to 60 miles holds— with great deal of trouble manage to erect tent— wind again strengthening the drift an hellish fright— decide to build break wind of snow blocks Bage & self two hours miserable work— 3 ft thick 15 ft long 5 ft high— now mid-night wind roaring past 75 miles— tent safe for time being at least— sledging under these God forsaken conditions sheer hell

25 November 1912

wild windage continuing through-out morning & all day about noon two snow petrels   we hail our little creatures with joy for they are the only living things in a fort-night   from whence they come or whither bound 80 miles inland on this plateau the last place in the world we expect they allow me a photograph my camera a bug-bear & using it a night-mare   every time I set shutter I have to take screws from front & bend mechanism into shape & with frostbit fingers!   we-do-not-stop sledging until 11PM it is now past mid-night & Jamaica shining brightly   the prospect without looking just like an ocean the crests of waves lit by Sun's golden glow & the great plateau i-n-e-x-p-r-e-s-s-i-b-l-y beautiful (Bage's pipe emits acrid fumes which he alone enjoys)

27 November 1912

we do not make start before 13 hrs 45 min & then in the teeth of a howling gale one must fight to gain e-v-e-r-y step the grey sastrugi standing full & square like tomb stones & a frigid wind stinging our faces it takes each atom of combined effort to win 4¼ miles the wind at 630PM up to 60 miles again & after hard day's toil we needs must build snow shelter before daring to erect tent in spite of conditions there is something grand & inspiring in treading these virgin snows & breaking trail FIRST TIME across the un-known & on-on-on we go over undulating ice plains whose surface is torn & swept by squalling as we top one rise another confronts us which we are just as anxious to conquer

29 November 1912

to-day the worst day every foot has to be won against relent-less tempest with strained stomach & bowed back at 107 miles our troubles increase & having to climb grade of about 1 in 40 with pitted frost surface swept with large & jagged sastrugi we become parched & try to quench our thirst by sucking ice which burns the tongue & affords small relief at camp time *dead beat* but break wind still to be built as environment bears evidence of more than ordinary severe wind Jamaica's rim just s-k-i-m-s the horizon then rapidly rises to shine upon the toils of another anxious day

3 December 1912

930AM & after HOOSHING haul sledge up South ridge of nodules here an amazing field of enormous crevasses we link together with Alpine rope for Tour of exploration many fissures 70 ft wide & spanned by great bridges of compressed snow some which have fallen & lie jammed below the whole place resembling land cut up into allotments & criss crossed by crevasses in every direction peering down one of these man traps we look into black nothingness the walls delicately festooned with the most beautiful crystals imaginable light filtering through ice walls makes chasms glow faint blue & heightens effect of these sledging night-mares to take sledge over this chaos our next problem to-day is my day for leading so attached to long rope I venture across 20 snow bridges stamping & jumping well if they hold me during such manoeuvres perhaps they will hold my comrades

7 December 1912

I often wonder if ever this journey will be appreciated & is it worth-while three hours hard toil we only cover 2½ miles as I make this entry it is blowing "GREAT GUNS" & the drift swishing against cotton walls we are frightfully cold & shiver ourselves warm three hours toil only 2½ miles the drift heavy the light so bad we can-not see where to place feet one is frightfully cold & shivers our wet socks & stockings pushed up our jerseys the light so bad we can-not see our feet it is snowing & blowing as to make further headway intolerable socks & stockings up our jerseys here the body warmth prevents them from freezing snowing & blowing our wet & frozen Burberrys spread over sleeping-bags here the body warmth prevents them freezing we build large break wind 6 ft 6 high x 30 feet wide an effectual shelter from wind & wet & sledging in Adelie Land is indeed without parallel a large break wind effectual shelter we travel in blizzards as normal conditions sledging in Adelie Land blowing "GREAT GUNS" against thin tent walls this journey is it really worth-while

15 December 1912

yesterday's severe pull not as severe as to-day the temp well below Zero & this with fierce wind makes life nigh intolerable but this is not all before we have bad surfaces either sastrugi or soft virgin snow & now we have both the light too bad we keep stumbling along over razor blade ridges or floundering through pie crust snow our breaths freeze in accumulated masses around helmets & cement our beards to-day has been one long struggle the marvel no broken limbs or serious injury yesterday's pull not as severe as to-day five days to go before turning "home"

19 December 1912

I take back all I said about harsh weather— to-day Heavenly perfectly cloud-less & calm the temperature in tent 66° & the black bulb thermometer 107.5° in the Sun! I always said this is a humorous country— sledging terrifically hot what with snow & Sun glare & us mightily glad to strip & haul in our shirts what characters we look! be-goggled & whiskered faces nearly black with Sun-burn & frostbite— an absolute hush broods over plateau broken only by c-r-e-a-k of runners gliding upon wind polished surfaces— we cover 14 miles a total of 282 from Hut & 18 more before we turn back— 11PM heavy banks of nimbus roll up from the South I darn my mits & pray our journey concludes

21 December 1912

to-day the most momentous since leaving Hut. by 3PM we reach 301 miles Latitude 70.37 Long 148.13. ours has been a difficult task hauling dead in the eye of the wind. still it's done & we feel our best has been done. with feelings half glad half regretful we turn back. behind us lie interminable ridges & personally I must say the lure of this region is strong & the vacant places still beckon irresistibly. we all feel sad for something seems to call us back eager to unfold to a distant world the mysteries of count-less ages. yet it is not to be. food will run out by 15th Jany. the Aurora will be waiting & then home again to Sunny lands & dear faces. Webb calculates position about 45 miles from South Magnetic Pole. 45 miles. at Turnback Camp we hoist sail on sledge & in less than an hour cover 2½ miles to last night's camp. no more shall we face the blizzard nor toil up steep ice slopes. the winds shall be fair & help us on our way yet it will be no picnic. what took us many weeks must now take only days.

22 December 1912

commence flight from 298 mile camp at 10AM & wind being favourable set off at great pace the area of sail about 49 square ft too much for the blowing which necessitates Webb & self situating behind & holding it back with guy ropes even then find hard to keep sledge from overrunning Bage that sledge! it appears more anxious to get home than us! eventually compelled to reef sail so with load just balanced we make good speed 18½ miles with little more exertion than walking & feeling right proud of our craft as she glides majestically over the polished sastrugi & very beautiful she looks with white wings out spread like a tiny barque on a frozen sea the sastrugi ranging 20 to 30 ft long & 4 to 5 ft high their forms very diverse great clam shells ocean rollers schools of porpoises each phenomenal shape due to wind action ablation attrition of drift particles we pick up old tracks & pass former camping spots places of cherished memories that mark like pillars of victory our mastery over the wild

25 December 1912

the following menu concocted from a half dozen ingredients tediously separated from compounded sledging ration—   Horsdoeuvre "Angels on gliders" (one raisin placed on top of bar of chocolate previously fried) Entree "Biscuit fried in sledging suet"   Main "Frizzled pemmican on fried biscuit"   Piece de resistance "Extra thick & greasy sledging ration" Sweets "Plum pudding" (3 grated biscuits/sugar/7 raisins/3 drops Meth all mixed with snow & boiled in sock 5 minutes)   we brew a strange drink of fire the "STINGO" recipe of one BOB BAGE as distasteful as its appearance & can only be drunk in gulps by holding one's nose & breath   no doubt our King would be greatly amused at the grimaces with which we drink his Health   still there is loyalty & sincerity amongst the men that sledge the plateau & our cheers could not be more hearty if celebrated with Champagne indeed I never knew a more jolly Xmas than this one spent with Bob Bage & Azzi Webb at "LUCKY DEPOT" 200 miles on the plateau

5 January 1913

(2AM) weather again over-cast which precludes us taking observation for Latitude— walk 4 miles in direction we anticipate Depot should lie but owing to atrocious light observe nothing— turn into sleeping-bags to keep warm & rations being short resolve to cut to half— now have sufficient to last about two days— things looking "exciting" for under prevailing weather conditions one might as well try to find grain of gold amongst desert sands— nought to do but see what the morrow brings forth

7 January 1913

to-day light as bad as ever snow all night & stagnantly calm *Heaven only knows where the Depot lies* keep in bags until 530PM then ¼ ration Hoosh the first for 17 hours strike camp 630PM move East along Latitude 67.57 Sth light so bad nothing beyond slatey expanse of snow & sky *Heaven only knows where Depot lies* things now serious one day's ration & one choice left remain here to gambol with weather OR make mad dash for Hut if-we-stay-&-things-do-not-clear as good as dead we die *Heaven only knows* hold consultation & determine should out look be bad on morrow to make quick bid for Hut our desperate yet only chance for Hut remains 70 miles away & trail runs through blizzard both surface & sky to Heaven knows where? we move off 6AM

9 January 1913

as much as we can do to force ourselves out of sleeping-bags this
morning Webb looks bad I suppose Bage & self look the same we decide
we must make 5 miles to West & then down to coast on this route we
find ourselves in badly crevassed & serraced ice bridged with snow
bridges which give way beneath us & precipitate us at the end of our
harness into abysmal depths towards mid-day we recognise great ice cliffs
of Commonwealth Bay & a few hours later the Mackellar Islets & at mid-
night "5 Mile" Depot it seems our very eyes must be lying what touches
most is the hand grip we give each other & the sight of dog biscuits we
crawl into "Five Mile" excavation & after Hoosh sleep sounder than for
months

10 January 1913

we leave "5 Mile" Depot at noon to-day   poor Bob's eyes have to be
bandaged as he is stone blind   we haul him on the sledge & have an
exciting time preventing it from capsizing into crevasses   at 5PM we
come down the long ice slope at the back of the Hut   those in the Hut
come out running & cheering   we have a Royal reception & are carried
into the Hut where Good Old Close has a banquet prepared   although
we-do-not-reach the Magnetic Pole we know our records are UNIQUE
& will comprise some of the most valuable scientific assets of this the
"Great Expedition"

THE SHACKLETON EXPEDITION

November 1914–September 1916

a day

5 November 1914—   often during the Mawson Expedition I
had the desire to visit South Georgia but little anticipated I was
so soon to observe its mist bound coast climb its jagged ranges
on the morning of 5th November our tenth day from leaving
Buenos Ayres the obscure outlines of a rugged & mountainous
coast are dimly observed through snow squalls & immediately
to the South unable to accurately determine a harbour entrance
in the mist we are pleasurably surprised to notice making in our
direction a small craft which on coming along-side proves to be
the Sitka a whaler from Leith Harbour Captain Michelson her
able skipper pilots us to Cumberland Bay where the Endurance
lays anchor in a superb miniature haven viz King Edward Cove

about whaling—   apart from the transcending scenery one is
at once struck by the pungent effluvium & noisesome aromas
which hang obscure yet fluid like over its greasy waters this is
an emanation from Grytviken Whaling Station & innumerable
derelict whale carcasses that float in the vicinity the Company
owns a flotilla of four whalers which scout seven days a week
patrolling a circuit of fifty miles from land on the sighting of a
whale from the crows nest a vessel will then steer in pursuit &
by judicious manoeuvring approach to within 30 or 40 yds of
the quarry the Skipper on the bow stands alert with harpoon
fitted with percussion head & when within range sights & fires
one follows the flight of the whizzing coiling rope as it runs at
great speed & then TAUGHTENS as the huge fish suddenly
explodes

a night

5 November 1914—— dine with some other members at Mr Jacobsen's & am agreeably surprised with its interior kept artificially heated about "incubation" heat it sports billiard table piano & real live geraniums the dinner table graced with spot-less linen so unlike our four week old stain absorbers & tastefully be-decked with a splendid display of blue & gold Chinaware upon which basks a tempting & wondrous variety of "sliced sausage" dear to the Norwegian heart (or stomach) after regaling there-on we are informed it is manufactured locally its ingredients being whale meat & whale fed pig we epicures unanimous in praise of "wurst" until next day observe herd of aforesaid "pig ingredients" emerge from out a whale's bowel wherein they had just completed (if grunts are indicatory) a sumptuous gorge after-wards some of us no longer caring to dine with Mr Jacobsen

a snap

of South Georgia— I have many pleasant rambles & excursions
on the Island & each time more deeply impressed by its rugged &
wild mountains its serraced glaciers & beauteous fjords here one
can study sub-antarctic life with all its attendant charm giant petrels
penguins Cape pigeons Cape hens etc etc & herds of sea elephants
sea leopards & occasional Weddell seals our friend Rasmussen takes
partys of Expedition self included to far reaches of Moraine Fjord
& Nordenskjold Glacier I mention the fjord specifically on account
of the lasting impression I retain of it a narrow water-way extending
some two miles between escarped mountains where Nature admires
her work in a liquid mirror & at the head of the fjord three glaciers
that rise near the majestic base of Mount Paget (7000 ft) & whose
occasional boom & crash precede the dislodgment of icy fragments
the only sound that awakes its echoes such do I remember Moraine
Fjord with its cloud shrouded peaks & its tussock covered hill-sides

a day

7 December 1914——   numerous tabular bergs observed
many of them weather worn into gorgeous caves & vaults
a multitude of dissipating forms I sight the mist mantled
peaks of the South Sandwich Islands off starboard while
the faintest line of ice blinks on the Southern horizon an
Easterly course is set & shortly after 5PM the Endurance
baptizes her bow in the marginal outskirts of the Weddell
Sea a field composed for the most part of old weathered
floes & denuded berg fragments they grow rapidly denser
as to become almost impenetrable

a note

about the Endurance— we admire our sturdy little ship
which seems to take a delight in combating our common
enemy shattering the floes in grand style when she comes
in impact with them she stops dead s-h-i-v-e-r-i-n-g from
truck to kelson then almost immediately a long crack starts
from our bow into which we steam & like a wedge slowly
force it sufficiently to enable passage & thus it has been all
day

a day

24 December 1914— what vicissitudes are awakened twelve
months ago I was on board the Aurora blown out of Common-
wealth Bay Christmas Eve two years ago on the Adelie plateau
100 miles from the South Magnetic Pole three years ago escape
from wrecking on rocks at Caroline Cove favourable conditions
to-day the ice floes separated by large stretches of water through
which we are enabled to make full speed tortuous course spend
morning filling sacks with coal noon temp plus 33 noon position
Lat 64° 32 S Long 17° 12 W a run of 70 miles the past 24 hours

a day

25 December 1914— Lees presents us at breakfast with a neat
little packet of great utility a small carborundum knife sharpener
in honour of the day the ward-room made gay with flags & table
cloths turned inside out so as to hide their colour paper napkins
also add a homely café like air The Menu mock turtle soup white
bait jugged hare Xmas pudding mince pies crystallized figs dates
in the evening a sing song until 8PM & glorious Sun-set the Sun
just dipping below the horizon for an hour or so near mid-night

a month

December 1914— large number Adelies & several sea leopards observed— large number of ringed penguins follow ship's wake — Ross seal shot & skinned & all looking forward to seal steaks for breakfast— Sunday & a slack day average temp 30— very slow progress having re-entered fields of enormous floes all day we have been utilizing ship as battering ram— secure three emperors for larder— progress still slow— a day of no progress— held up all day by wind— crabeaters & one seal leopard noticed also a blue whale— uneventful day— beset by pack-ice temp falls to 21 at 6AM & freezes up loose brash & water spaces— no change in position— afraid unfavourable winds have set us back 19 miles

a day

1 January 1915—   see New Year in at wheel
under snowy conditions a few enthusiasts join
"Auld Lang Syne" but the majority all sound in
slumber during day have very gratifying run we
pass through vast fields of younger ice the ship
cuts her way in a noble style leaving wake to be
traced it remains open for a mile I have a plat-
form suspended from jibboom from whence I
secure Cine film & photos from a-top foretop
yard

a vista

of ocean— glorious morning & being on "washdown" have
full benefit of its exhilarating charm the water a dazzling deep
blue— the ocean has altered its tint from deep blue to light
bottle green due to presence of an immensity of diatomaceous
deposits I take a glimpse through Clarke's microscope of one
single drop & wonder of wonders to witness beautiful shapes
of these minute animalculae— bergs & floes reflected & the
heavy pressure ice gleaming in the Sun-shine with its deep blue
shadows one of the finest sights I have ever beheld— view
from mast head the surface has entirely altered ahead of ship it
appears as an immense chaos of hummocks & ridges piled up
in wildest confusion— huge fragments rounded by attrition
strew the fore shores the sea laden with broken blocks jostle &
crunch one another with a crackle like small artillery— early
morning greeted by open water I muse over this gladsome sight
thinking this same ocean breaking on these inhospitable shores
also tumbles its green Pacific rollers over the golden sands of
Manly

a night

23 January 1915—   this evening favoured with Sun-light
I climb up into barrel look out from where a magnificent
panorama observed from horizon to horizon & stretching
North South East West the pack-ice extends dazzling white
relieved by long shadows the sight very inspiring & makes
one feel their tininess & insignificance the Endurance the
only black speck amid eternal whiteness is thrown in weird
skeleton fashion far across snows by a Heavenly mid-night
Sun

a snap

take photographs of dogs feeding etc—   under-way 230AM
we enter long leads of ice free water in which drift some bergs
MAGNIFICENT forms one a fine cuniform mass 200 ft high
I photograph it—   am awakened during night towards mid-
night to take more photos the mid-night Sun shining brilliant
& as its low light tips the heavy pressure floes & ice the effect
very beautiful—   during day a phenomenal sight hundreds of
crabeaters gambolling sporting & diving under ship for over a
quarter of an hour I have rare opportunity of securing Cinema
of this extra-ordinary sight—   to-day a glorious Sunny day I
take advantage of same to secure a number of natural colour
plates—   experiment with Paget Autochrome—   day spent
developing using ship's refrigerator for dark-room a miserable
occupation

a month

January 1915— uneventful day— another attempt South-
ward only to find pack has walled-us-in so forced back North-
ward— in the midst of impenetrable field & heavy pressure
ice— this ice a consolidated field of hummocks HIGHER
at times than our bulwarks— a notable day the first glimpse
of Coate's Land 520PM— I start reading "Guinea Gold" by
Beatrice Grimshaw— finish reading "Gold" by Grimshaw—
tied up all day to floe ice— magnificent day the finest since
leaving South Georgia in fact the second Sunny day we have
had— I start reading Marcus Clarke's "For the Term of His
Natural Life"— compulsorily hove-to weathering in lee of
ice berg Sunday at best a lazy day— finish reading Clarke's
exquisite book it impresses me greatly especially since I have
visited various places around which his tale is woven— un-
interesting day held up in pack-ice— reading excerpts from
"Human Boy" by Phillpotts— held up in the pack— large
crabeater secured for larder— still held up— still held by
ice— nothing of any moment takes place— start reading
"Idols" by Locke— 15 days held up in pack immovable—
the life on deck trying the weather stagnant not even an "ear"
of wind

a day

5 February 1915—   an amusing argument at breakfast
concerning a much debated question about a monkey &
a pole which provokes much heated & facetious debate
we are surprised at noon by a violent shock which upon
investigation shows the cracking up of our floe the crack
extending the breadth of the floe & our ship being in its
direct path hearty cheers go up as all hands rush on deck
to witness this joyous happening "THE RELEASE OF
OUR SHIP" after being frozen in nearly three weeks our
joy however short lived as the floe comes together again
& we are in precisely the same predicament as we were in
before

a note

about ice— during morning I go for stroll to old
lead ahead which is now nearly 1 ft thick I am much
interested in examining the contexture of recent ice
the growth commencing by formation of small fish-
scale like crystals accumulating without any definite
orientation in horizontal layers this formation then
extending below surface for half an inch where the
plate crystals gradually arrange themselves vertically
probably due to the heavier saline solution sinking &
thus directing automatically the disposition of plates
the accretion then continuing by increment of these
vertical scales the young ice fracturing at right angles
to its plane & subsequently under-going further re-
crystallization

a vista

of whales— splendid view of two killers poking their
alligator like heads through new ice astern & blowing
arduously more villainous rapacious looking creatures I
have never seen— fine view of two killers gambolling
in adjacent lead gazing admiringly with "sad eyes" poor
hungry creatures I don't think— skis are indispensable
cracks 4 & 5 feet frequently to be crossed & negotiation
forces one to develop a cat like gentleness of tread it is
astonishing the speed one can travel should a killer poke
his head through the ice what curious bosom sensations
it excites!— frequently find self a-float on small floes
& needs must use skis for paddles this novel method of
ferrying I quickly abandon owing to visions of attack by
killers their presence being indicated by un-distant snorts
& blows— many killers now in adjacent pools one can
hear their blowing last night I observed school of seven
dorsals sporting— the incessant blowing I may simile
to a railway yard choc full of engines blowing off at high
pressure

a day

11 February 1915— engines unable to move us
out of soft floe in which we are jammed at 9AM
engines put full astern & we "sally ship" that is all
hands & Cook at given signal double over to port
then starboard & so on imparting a rolling motion
to ship so forcing her to split surrounding young
ice if unsuccessful all hands muster on poop & in
rhythmic time jump up jump down such sallying
provoking much hilarity but having desired effect
& ship re-moored to take advantage of any viable
opening

a note

about dogs—   ten exercised in harness to-day first lesson
since leaving Hudson Bay three in extremely bad condition
have to be shot—   dogs placed on shore much to delight
all hands engaged in building "dogloos" from blocks of ice
the dogs secured by chain one end of which is buried in ice
& frozen therein by the simple action of pouring water—
canine tuition only successfully accomplished by frequent
& judicious application of whip served up with a stringent
vocabulary—   "Mush!" team moves forward as single unit
"Gee!" leader turns left about 30° "Haw!" causes leader to
adopt right-ward course "Hup-there!" assisted by explicit
adjectives causes team to increase gait & a long drawn out
"Woah!" brings them to rest—   my own team led by old
Shakespeare finest of pack along with Bob ardent worker
who gives me no trouble Rugby friendly inclined although
minus wagging extremity Rufus venerable quadruped has
seen better days Hakensmidt good puller the size of a calf
then Noel the smallest & Jerry & Martin brothers & lastly
Sailor capricious rascal & cunning apparently exerting while
rest of team working—   each dog is capable of drawing
100lbs—   on leaving Buenos Ayres we have 69 dogs the
mortality very heavy only 54 left (besides the 8 little pups)

a snap

anxious to develop Cinema film & I spend
the day in dark-room— whilst at weekly
custom scrubbing alley-way a tack passing
through one finger incapacitates me from
photographic work a short while— have
packed & unpacked my cases several times
barometrically with the ship's condition in
the ice— quite a run of sitters to-day for
"portraiture"

a night

23 February 1915—   the Sun comes out after tea & all turn out
to indulge in strenuous game of Hockey it is a charming evening
the atmosphere charged with a redundancy of shimmering frost
crystals & a magnificent parhelion two fragments of a 22° halo
forming around Sun the lower sections being visible right down
to horizon & two well developed mock Suns with an extension
of light directed away from the Sun on this ring a faint section of
an arc 46° above Sun the characteristic Sun pillar is well marked
& terminates in tapering extremity 15° above the solar disc 8PM

a day

5 March 1915—   a line of mounds marking a track to the lead ahead &
a wide circle around ship erected by sailors with wire hawser stretched
connecting them together these to act as guides for those straying from
ship in blizzard times during morning a striking recurrence of parhelion
exceeding in brilliancy & colour all previously witnessed the atmosphere
replete with scintillating rime crystals which under examination exhibit
modifications of the hexagon the solar disc appearing as nebulous glare
surrounded by two concentric circles with radii 22° & 46° whose lower
circumferences lie below horizon displaying the well defined red of the
spectrum on their inner edge & exterior green with mock Suns devoid
of colour two coloured tangential arcs intersecting the circles along their
vertical axis the lower assuming wavy formation this impressive display
lasting several hours waxing waning & assuming fragmentary alterations
proportional to intensity of rime crystals with which the atmosphere is
charged

a note

about seals—   they emerge from junctions
or cracks in the floe to Sun themselves lazily
in the warm lea of hummocks & to sleep off
the somniferous effects of over-feeding one
may sit & study them from but several yards
distance when they will gaze drowsily stretch
luxuriously & yawn & fall off to sleep again
ashore the Weddell is THE most phlegmatic
creature I know of his very shape resembling
a gigantic slug suggests both sloth & lassitude
but the water is his element & I have watched
him gliding superbly or sporting in the leads
the perfection of sinuous grace poor creature
how unfortunate for you that your flesh is so
e-x-c-e-l-l-e-n-t & your blubber burns so well

a night

6 March 1915— during evening a singing musical competition
takes place the prize being unanimously awarded to Sir Ernest his
voice is quaint vacillating between sharps & flats in a most unique
manner Wordie now ex-champion renders "The Gambolier" in a
voice resembling the shrill tone caused by drawing a rasp smartly
across an edge of galvanized iron then Clark with much applause
"My Nut Brown Maiden" in a nasal super tenor & I contribute old
favourite "Waltzing Matilda" in the melting dulcet tones one often
hears from a swaggie crooning at Sun-set when punching his frugal
damper it is quite astonishing the musical talent we do not possess

a snap

of Rampart Berg—   it is located some eight miles South of the
ship & on account of its irregular form is very pictorial we leave
the ship 8AM hauling a light sledge carrying photographic gear
& Hoosh—   this colossal block of ice has a base of some 300
acres & raises its crenellated towers 180 feet above the sea along
its top surface immense battlemented embrasures the open ends
of crevasses that give the appearance of a Titanic fortification &
around its base the pack-ice rafts & groans complainingly being
goaded along as the monster ploughs with majesty through it—
standing on the rafting pressure we make the blue caverns echo
with hearty "Coo-ees" & after securing pictures we return to ship
an excellent tea & sleep

a month

April 1915— no further hope being entertained of ship breaking out
this Season— blowing a full gale with snow drift clearing gangs remove
loads of snow from ship's vicinity & evacuate the dogs— observe Sun
to-day by refraction probably last glimpse til coming spring— observe
fine paraselene Lat 75° 16 S Long 44° 11 W temp −12— Sadie gives
birth to pup in the night which closely resembles a guinea-pig— secure
twenty emperors the birds in fine plumage & condition several scaling
85lbs we induce them out of lead by making an imitatory croaking noise
which attracts them right up to ship— rigging encrusted with hard rime
giving appearance of a Christmas card ship covered all over with glass

a snap

20 March 1915— during evening I give illustrated lantern lecturette on Java & across Australia all hands after-guard & fo'c'sle roll up to a man it is quite a relief to see some tropical vegetation & flowers even though they are but shadowgraphs projected on a screen 17 April 1915— after customary weekly toast for sweet-hearts & wives the "Ritz" again rigged as lecture room where I display slides of Mawson Expedition 15 May 1915— give third series of lantern lectures on New South Wales to which all attend 10 July 1915— final lantern lecture on New Zealand I allow Worsley to lecture he being a native New Zealander he speaks uneloquently his accounts all confined to *It is − er − er − so & so* however he retrieves himself by executing a Maori war-dance

a day

15 June 1915—   great fancy dress gathering & betting to-day
on Antarctic Derby Stakes all available chocolate & cigarettes
the local currency brought into requisition Sir Ernest is starter
& line near ship is "Home" the day opens dull & over-cast the
track visible only by hurricane lamps the "Khyber Pass" light
flashes its signal to GO! & the teams are OFF! great cheering
ensues the dogs joining in with wild barking Wild's team seen
racing down track then come Macklin's & McIlroy's headed by
Bony Peter the drivers urge with shouts & varied vocabularies
Wild wins race in 2 minutes 16 seconds with Hurley coming in
second

a snap

owing to fallen temperature it being −19 a heavy condensation
develops on cameras when brought aboard I have made a cup-
board on deck where they can be kept at an even temperature
nevertheless the apparatus needs attention every time it is taken
out lubricating with petroleum etc especially the Cinematograph
under these extremes the film becomes extremely brittle & loses
about 10% sensitiveness—   a form of mid-winter madness has
manifested itself all hands being seized with the desire to have
their hair removed & luxuriant curls bald pates & parted crowns
soon became akin we are likely to be cool headed in the future
if not neuralgic we resemble a cargo of convicts & I do not let
opportunity pass of perpetuating photographically this humorous
happening—   after three attempts I succeed in securing flash-
light of my team being fed the charges of flash power placed in
three shielded receptacles & fired electrically the dogs extremely
scared—   arise early & secure some pictures in natural colour
of magnificent Sun-rise—   clear afternoon Worsley & self go
picture stalking he being used most effectively as prop to include
in pictures so that the size of surrounding objects may be gauged

a night

30 June 1915— my turn to night-watch the duties of
night-watch are to keep the "Ritz" bogie glowing the
"Stables" roasting & the Boss's room which is right aft
at an equable temperature the latter is a difficult job as
temperature within is either 90° or well below freezing
according to the vicissitudes of the wind & Sir Ernest's
temper reciprocates in kind the night-watch also rouses
others & they sit in quorum around bogie discoursing
in subdued whispers & partaking of his homage to wit
sardines on toast a great favourite grilled biscuit cocoa
or tea & the visitors termed "ghosts" well appreciative

a note

about dogs— they are exercised at noon but it is very difficult
to find one's way about so I leave it to old Shakespeare to nose
his way home which he does without trouble it is magnificent to
watch him picking the better tracks & away we go jumping over
pressure ridges holes ice stumps I have added two extra runners
to my sledge & supplemented bow by one made from a pipe the
result most efficient I have christened it the Dreadnought poor
Rufus oldest member of my team dies of bronchial pneumonia
Macklin's team falls into ice lead he has great trouble extricating
them the cold air freezing the hair of the dogs together as a pack
Clark secures an emperor rounded up by Sue's two pups I have
another race with Wild Wild comes in pulling 910lbs in just two
minutes 9 seconds my team same weight 7 seconds later but Sir
E falls off Wild's sledge & Wild is disqualified so winner is one
"Frank Hurley"

a snap

take colour cameras to lead again this morning amidst similar
gorgeous conditions of yesterday more glorified perhaps for a
fine crop of ice flowers have sprung up resembling a field of
pink carnations—   during night take flash-light of ship beset
by pressure this necessitates some 20 flashes one behind each
salient hummock half blinded by successive flashes I lose my
bearings bumping shins against projecting ice points stumbling
into deep snow drifts pack quiet but away to the North clouds
of sea smoke rise like distant fire—   low temperature renders
dark-room work extremely difficult it being −13 washing plates
a most troublesome operation as tank must be kept warm or
plates enclose into block of ice after several changes of water I
place them in rack in Sir E's cabin at fairly equable temperature
the dry plates then all spotted & carefully indexed development
a source of much pain to fingers which crack & split all around

a month

June 1915— the darkest part of the year— two hours poor
twilight very dim at noon— no animal life observed— stars
of the 5th magnitude observed at noon— eerie sounds of ice
pressure a faint booming groaning creaking— bitterly cold &
no-one allowed away from ship— all day the wind screams in
rigging— blizzard conditions all day— ice works grinding
away on starboard bow in fine style we are very apprehensive it
will come closer— four emperors secured— first time in 79
days Old Jamaica peeps above the horizon & after winking but
a minute then sets in glowing majesty firing up sky with crimson
[*Nor dim nor red / Like God's own Head / The glorious Sun uprist*]

a note

about ice—   a diligent watch maintained an hourly watch kept
during night a crack starts from lead ahead & runs to within 30
yards of Endurance about 400 yards ahead the ice is very active
crunching & rafting huge fragments weighing many tons being
forced up & balanced on top of pressure ridges over 15 ft high
frequent patches of water emit dense volumes of frost-smoke a
pellicule of ice forming almost immediately when lead opens up
I take interesting walk amongst the hummocks inspecting shape
theorising on form such diversified pinnacles & fractures need
a more able pen than mine to describe but what impresses most
i-m-m-e-n-s-e piles of ground ice caused by attrition of Titanic
floes the sail area presented to winds by millions of hummocks
& thousands of square miles of ice must develop a power quite
profound

a night

22 August 1915—   beautiful alpengluhen on pack
at Sun-rise I walk ahead of ship the water all calm &
pink tinted pinnacles bounding the margin reflected
within Sir E joins me & together we walk treading
fairy-land the pack to the South a grotesquely rosey
shade a peculiar miraging of distant bergs & the air
so exhilarating one can scarce refrain from bursting
into song

a night

2 September 1915—   heavy pressure to-night
I anticipate the beams along-side my bunk will
splinter then the floor in the "Ritz" buckles in
alarming manner & the partition between ours
& Lee's cubicle springs tongue from groove &
one can-not but feel apprehensive when a deck
begins opening under one's feet & you hear it
groaning beneath this embrace I do not mind
getting out stretching my legs despite the land
being 300 miles away but do prefer when the
temperature warmer it presently being just 53°
below

a month

September 1915— uneventful— toast sweet-hearts & wives
as per custom— uneventful day— cold & bleak with drifting
snow but two emperor penguins caught— salinity insitu sample
of top 2½" surface freshly formed ice 13.1 per thousand sample
of water salinity 34.7 per thousand— ice conditions quiescent at
present— ice quiet to-day— ice utterances away to the South
nought to note beyond refraction & over-cast sky— Wild shoots
seal the FIRST since winter— Wild & McIlroy bring in female
shot on 24th— Wild shoots additional bull the seals welcome as
dog biscuits running out— Clark observes slight increase of life
in plankton net— snow petrel first sign of winged life returning
flies past Endurance North-wards— day cloudy with heavy rime
precipitation— five crabeaters secured two with well developed
foetis— two very accommodating seals waddle up to within 80
yards of ship & in consequence secured for larder— during the
month James has made series of interesting observations & tests
by the silver nitrate method to determine structural phenomenon
I subtend the following data—

a day

15 October 1915— my twenty-eighth birthday at mid-
night the Endurance drifts from her cradle where she has
been frozen & falls astern leaving her form moulded in
the splintered floe behind her the sparker is hoisted & we
actually sail 100 yards our first movement since Feb 15th
we are now in a path double the width of ship's beam &
blocked immediately ahead by a narrow transverse lead
our position I review with some anxiety as we inevitably
must be severely nipped should the floes come together
a whale makes his appearance in lead behind ship during
day while temp falls from plus 31° to plus 3° the ice not
showing any inclination to disintegrate in current vicinity

a night

17 October 1915—   the ice seems intent on disturbing our
Sunday evening Gramophone concerts as it invariably sets up
a whining & "gets busy" punctual to 6PM we hear the dreaded
groaning followed almost immediately by the vessel vibrating
as though trembling with fear at the oncoming conflict it is a
cracky un-even conflict for together arrive the vice like floes &
grip the ship as she shivers & creaks but ever more relent-less
the grip & when we expect her sides to stave in she s-l-o-w-l-y
rises up from the pressure at this critical juncture it suddenly
eases her stern forced 3 feet 4 inches out of the ice & then she
assumes her normal position so much for our musical pleasure

a vista

of pressure— every timber straining to rupture— decks
gape— doors refuse to open or shut— iron floor plates
in engine room bulge & spring from seatings— everything
in a state of extreme compression— we begin to rise from
the ice like a pip between fingers— in the space of seconds
we are SHOT from the floes & thrown over to port with list
of 30°— great is the chaos dogs kennels sledges men all an
inextricable tangle— oncoming floe impinges against helm
& soundings in well announce gloomy tidings we are rapidly
making water— pumps clickety clack— a huge pressure
ridge menaces starboard quarter & astern— the position is
serious— highly precarious— it is evident our enemy will
not remain passive— I pack my album in waterproof cloth
it being the only record I shall be able to save if compelled to
take to the floe

a day

26 October 1915—   I shall ever remember this afternoon
I am assisting Chips caulking coffer dam when the pressure
sets in the groaning of timbers mingling with crunching ice
producing hideous din the dogs instinctively conscious of
imminent peril set up distressed wails of uneasiness & fear
Sir E calmly surveys movements of ice at 6PM the pressure
increases amidst these profound & over-whelming forces we
are the absolute embodiment of help-less futility at 7PM the
order is given to lower the boats the boats are hauled some
distance away away from the Endurance & out of immediate
danger

a vista

of disintegration— we have just finished Hoosh & the "ice mill"
in motion again— closer & closer approaches the pressure wave
like a huge frozen surf— immense slabs raft up to its crest which
topple down & are over-ridden by a chaos of crunched fragments—
this stupendous power marches ever onward grinding away through
the 5 ft floe surrounding our staunch little craft— now it is within
a few yards & the vessel groans & quivers I am quickly down on the
moving ice with Cinematograph expecting every minute to witness
the springing & buckling sides stave in— the line of pressure now
assaults the ship & she is borne into the crown of its ridge— the
pumps work faster & faster & someone is singing a "shanty" to their
beat— the dogs are passed down a canvas chute & secured on the
floe followed by cases & cases of rations sledges & equipage— all
hands assemble in ward-room to partake of final dinner aboard the
good ship the meal taken in silent gravity whilst crushing in progress
& ominous sounds arise from below— Sir E hoists blue ensign to
three lusty cheers & is last to leave— by some curious happening
the emergency light switches on off on off this intermittent making
& breaking of its circuit seems to transmit a final signal of fare-well

a day

28 October 1915—   temperature falls to 47° below
temporary tents struck & removed three times due to
the floe splitting beneath them we are approximately
350 miles from Paulette Island winter quarters of the
Nordenskjold Expedition here there awaits a store of
provisions it is intended a party should sledge across
ocean ice & endeavour to communicate with whaling
factory at Wilhelmina Bay or Deception Harbour the
floes in high state of agitation through-out day I have
Cinema trained on ship the whole time near evening
secure unique film of her masts collapsing as though
conscious of having achieved their purpose & the ice
quiescent again

a snap

of ephemera—   the dump heap a heterogeneous
collection of dress suits hats portmanteaus combs
brushes gold studs sovereigns books etc pleasant
though use-less refinements of civilization after all
value is but relative—   poor ship what a battered
wreck she now is—   the starboard side crushed in
& cabins all along closed up efficiently as a folding
"Kodak"

a note

about our camp—   the general appearance reminds one
of an Alaskan mining settlement in winter viz in the centre
surrounded by piles of stores is the eating House belching
from chimney a trail of brown smoke that has already left
its trade-mark across the snow the tents are arranged in a
row with the huskies pegged out in respective teams while
around us lies a vast illimitable Champagne of snow which
not even the most fertile imagination could conceive to be
the frozen bosom of the sea it is beyond conception even
to us that we dwell on a colossal ice raft with but 5 feet of
ice separating us from two thousand fathoms of ocean we
drift along under caprice of wind & tides to Heaven knows
where?

a day

30 October 1915—— raw snowy morning Sir E announces the
march will begin at 7PM a start is made the plan of procession
being as follows a path finding party of three precedes advance
with light sledge & demolishes hummocks & bridge cracks &
smooths out track then seven sledges each drawn by seven dogs
loaded 100lbs per dog then five teams return bring up balance
of gear loaded onto five sledges Wild's & mine own team to link
together & bring up light boat the remaining eighteen members
to manhaul large boat the James Caird after 2½ hours a halt is
made with about one mile traversed but all in high hopes & glad
to be finally gone from depressing neighbourhood of the wreck

a snap

during morning go on board & bring off in triumph
a number of tooth-brushes & paste I have to beat a
hasty retreat owing to portentous creaking on leaving
I take final look at dark-room wherein is submerged
my treasured negatives & instruments—   during day
I hack through thick walls of refrigerator to retrieve
negatives stored therein they are located beneath four
feet of mushy ice & stripping to waist & diving under
I haul them out—   spend afternoon with Sir Ernest
selecting finest of negatives from year's collection I
resolder up 120 & dump around 400 this unfortunate
reduction essential as a drastic cutting down in weight
must be affected owing to limited space in the boats

a note

about my comrades—   there is very curious attire in the camp
our general aspect deserving of comment viz hirsute visages &
variegated garb I will delineate a few of the salient types—   he
with the patch-work trousers & torn shooting jacket booted like
a Titan & hatted with wide Sun-hat like a boundary rider is your
"humble"—   the gentleman with very soiled evening dress-suit
black hands negroid face & perspiring over sooty blubber range
is Green the Cook—   attired like a show-man in coat of many
skins & cracking whip ostentatiously over his team is Marston—
next Wild woolly of mein always minus head gear or mits—   &
then the others inveterately clad in Burberrys with draught-board
seated breeches & aged coats still sporting proudly their rows of
buttons—   we are a motley crowd a reversion to the prehistoric
both in face & habit yet happy as larks & hopeful for a "future"
together

a night

31 December 1915— many sweet memories crowd on me
as I lie in sleeping-bag meditating on the last day of the year
home faces places & our present condition that one can-not
altogether regard as "sweet" drifting about on an ice floe 189
miles from land still "it might be worse" & inside tents all are
comfortable Sir E thinking & solving his magic squares New
Year resolutions we have none to make as there is nothing to
make them for un-less it be to keep those Hoosh pots cleaner

a month

December 1915—   four crabeaters secured—   made spoon
from bit of an oar—   boats practically finished only awaiting
opening of ice—   two emperor penguins secured this evening
for larder—   mid-night Sun observed for first time—   four
whales secured—   lazy day in tent reading Encyclopaedia on
Borneo Sumatra Australia—   three seals secured & eight bottle
necked whales gambol in lead—   weather dull no observations
play Elimination in bags—   all hands in tents to-day blizzard
conditions—   Hudson & Boss engage in heated argument on
overmastering power of love—   while-away day reading from
"Britannica" this magnificent work the greatest save from ship—
two Adelie penguins five Antarctic petrels observed—   reading
"Rope Manufacture"—   cold SSW wind with intermittent drift
all day all hands under canvas—   young crabeater captured—
now 234 miles from Paulette Island having drifted 120 miles on
floes from wreck of Endurance—   a fat Weddell seal also one
crabeater secured fresh meat is ever at our door—   foul wind
from NE all day bleak & in tents—   start "Nicholas Nickelby"
—   pass large plains of diatom coloured ice—   two partys set
out during day for seals six secured of which I find & kill three

a day

14 January 1916—   during morning four teams of dogs shot
Messrs Wild's Crean's McIlroy's & Marston's comprising total
thirty magnificent sledgers this step having been given lengthy
consideration the dogs are of no further use to us especially in
view of rarity of seals & our consequent inability to feed them
the decision a wise one the dogs consume one seal per day the
same lasting entire party three days during afternoon my team
shot a sad but unfortunate necessity Hail to thee Shakespeare
fear-less faithful old leader ever ready to thy Master's bidding

a vista

of superstitions— I have just walked around tent
three times being prescribed method of exorcising
evil wind spirits— the evil omened effect of salt-
spilling must be annulled by throwing a pinch over
left shoulder— wind spoken of with reverence &
wood must be touched when commenting thereon
— days of the month the 7th or factors thereof
are thought of as lucky whilst all precautious of the
13th— we cling to or concoct theories regarding
cyclones & anticlones mostly incorrect for which I
am thankful otherwise we would be existing amidst
dolldrums & eddies that would certainly baffle all
efforts of the floe to free us from our icy confines

a day

26 January 1916—   o life of change-less monotony
& idleness how dreary thy hours same scenery same
daily actions same routine walks & food one wearies
even of same faces droll witticisms theories & topics
almost exclusively appertaining to "currents" "winds"
thus we have lived unvaryingly NINETY DAYS on
the floe drifting with the elements still hope enables
us to forbear with patience & sweet fancy gives wing
to many a slow beat hour let us continue to hope the
ice will dessimate & who knows but Heaven it may?

a month

January 1916— playing this game of wait is wearing down everyone's patience we might as well wait for the ocean to melt up— confined to tent all day— misty snowy rainy with adverse winds— weather stagnant— have monthly wash FACE ONLY— numerous Adelie penguins waddle into camp & are potted— Poker Patience scores Sir EHS = 1100 JFH = 1095— re-reading Browning— morning spent manufacturing cribbage board— re-read Keats read "Golden Treasury of Verse"— Poker Patience scores Sir EHS = 1065 JFH= 1125— observe & kill one crabeater seal— Sir E & Hudson arguing religious matters— read Kinglake's "Eothen"— Poker Patience Sir EHS = 1090 JFH = 1110— miscellaneous encounters with seals secure two— come to end of "Eothen" I would rather carry this book than six times its weight in rations alas! the book now finished & round me remains the unchangable ice the same leaden sky the same white line that girdles the vision & acts like a bar to our frigid captivity but beyond that horizon lies the great rolling road to freedom & so we continue to hope

a note

about food—   Cook manufactures enormous bannock for lunch
good to eye but wafer like to appetite Antarctic etiquette permits
eating with fingers labiodental sounds are also permissible another
lunch Cook manufactures laudable rice cakes their prodigious bulk
appeases appetite of even No 5 tent a tent of capacious stomachs
& green eyes meals the most welcome times for then & only then
we endeavour to hold the fleeting minutes by slow mastication a
process which makes one feel at least mentally the repast ample we
sup this evening off hotchpot of remnant ingredients the flavour
not altogether pleasant but novel to palates all vitiated through re-
curring diet unsavoury lunch of eleven penguin hearts tough as old
boots theoretically should be feeling extremely bilious having just
regaled self of three penguin livers & two slices fatty ham fried in
seal blubber on the other hand found meal ambrosial & earnestly
spooned up oleaginous residue with contentment of a true epicure

a vista

of ice— the ice is rotting & one is on the alert at all intervals
lest he should break through into the Weddell Sea— ice very
honeycombed in places pools are showing through surface full
of euphausia & diatomaceous scum— examine icy expanse
with 12 magnification prisms from summit of Pinnacle Berg no
signs of life— this afternoon the pack illumined by pure Sun-
light dazzling beyond description the snow scintillating with a
pearl like lustre— from Flat Berg the prospect resembles an
immense plain bounded only by horizon of un-broken marble
littered thick with alabaster castles & ruins in every conceivable
form some like huge dirigibles others like sky scrapers temples
yachts etc some over-turned with bottom up others crevassed &
beautified as if that were possible with caverns draperies arches
of transparent icicles— this vastness of frozen water is slowly
drifting North where in warmer seas it would disperse fragment
by fragment til finally returning to its native element the ocean

a day

15 February 1916— camp temperament suffers a considerable
modulation by barometric vicissitudes when the glass falls heralding
advent of adverse winds a wave of tribulation & pessimism sweeps
through which immediately reverts to smile & song with favourable
barometer our icy barque devoid of helm & guidance propelled by
baffling winds is nought but a straw wisp in a whirl-wind responsive
to capricious gusts that blow from the Cardinal points & "box" the
compass under these irregular influences however we are not really
entitled to complain for since the ship's destruction the remarkable
drift of over 250 miles almost due course to Paulette Island has so
been accomplished without exertion or will this gives rise to a most
interesting paradox in the law of probabilities for if we are but one
floe of the millions constituting the Weddell Sea & being moved by
winds & currents from diverse directions what is the probability of
reaching a predetermined point 300 miles distant only Heaven can
know

a note

about hunting— five crabeaters & huge sea leopard secured the
latter chasing Lees around floe at great pace   I capture three seals
but have difficulty getting them in on account of drifting ice this
then results in a dream during which I am assailed by herd of crab-
eaters   I go a-hunting & rewarded by finding two fine seals which
I secure in orthodox manner rendering them insensible by a hit on
the nose with a ski then cutting their throats I hate such brutality
of method but they are remarkably tenacious of life   three coveys
of penguins trespass our floe & all hands muster en masse & with
loud "shillalahs" secure 68 prisoners skinned & refrigerated   skins
are reserved for fuel/legs for Hoosh/breasts for steaks & livers &
hearts for delicacies   I observe large covey of penguins too many
to cope with single-handed so semaphore camp & all armed with
cudgels turn out to give battle a bevy of 150 secured   follow false
scent for seal which turns out to be brace of penguins exterminate
60   take customary run to Flat Berg where sanguinary encounter
with massive Ross seal occurs   an hour later I ogle his steaks with
approval as they recline on Cook's table awaiting events of morrow

a month

February 1916— no news— reading Young's "Travels
in France"— Sir E introduces me to game of Piquet—
doing nothing beyond being patient— reading "The Sea
Captain" by Bailey— no news— snooze eat read play
cards wait— o! to be on land— finish "Sea Captain"
but not impressed therewith— to bed at 6PM nothing
else to do & Hoosh finished— reading "What I Saw in
Russia" by Hon Maurice Baring— spend time inventing
Antarctic equipment & innovations— cold & snowy—
read "The Making of the Earth" by JW Gregory— fair
wind all day— another day passed nil accomplished—
nothing doing— it now appears we shall remain another
winter in Antarctica— secure 3 Weddells & massacre
130 penguins— discuss flowers horticulture in sleeping-
bags— to dreams at 615PM— glad when day is over

a night

1 March 1916— wax poetical a magnificent
night with crystal clear atmosphere the moon
almost on horizon resembles the golden horn
of fairy tales pending in a lustrous firmament
bespangled with brilliants & one's imagination
running riot might conjecture a blast sounded
on horn will break the magic of this sight as
moon dips & faint orange blush suffuses its
path which broadens & glows til dawn spreads
with tints of pink & blue & the dissipation of
night's enchantment discloses immense pools
of still water surrounding our island floe from
which clouds of frost smoke lazily arise golden
in the rising Sun the beau ideal of our dreams

a snap

of the Boss— breakfast at 9AM sharp else
woe betide Sir Ernest's humour in morning
very erratic— have great admiration for the
Boss who is very considerate kindly disposed
an excellent comrade— Sir Ernest is very
interesting I enjoy hearing his extra-ordinary
experiences— Sir E recovering from attack
of rheumatics I apply mustard plaster which
causes much amusement especially striking
of its position— walk around floe with the
chief one of the finest characters I have ever
been fortunate to meet— discussion with
Sir E on polar & Expedition matters which I
heartily enjoy from these jaunts I learn much
of his excellent personality— Sir E I like
immensely he pictures to me Old England &
other lands whilst I speak of the "glories" of
my own & so the time passes— I especially
admire & sympathize with Sir E on whom the
entire brunt of responsibility & decisions fall
his indefatigable energy meticulous attention
for the party's safety merits thanks & approval
of all

a vista

of Poker Patience—   6 games for dinner not less than 10/–
or more than 15/– each Sir E 1110 JFH 1340—   for smokes
not to exceed 10/– Sir E 1110 JFH 1040—   for theatre stalls
10/6 each Sir E 1110 JFH 1045—   for new hat price 1 guinea
(Johnson Hatters 38 Bond Street) Sir E 1020 JFH 1040—   for
Umbrella price £1 Sir E 1210 JFH 1190—   £1 mirror v book
same value Sir E 940 JFH 1195—   Handkerchiefs v Ties to
value of £1/1 Sir E 1025 JFH 1165—   Duplex razors v book
Sir E 650 JFH 855—   Umbrella v £1/1 book Sir E 1070 JFH
1255—   Travelling Soap Box Sir E 1160 JFH 1170—   Tie
Case v Collar box Sir E 1090 JFH 1135—   for Clothes Brush
Sir E 1095 JFH 1245—   Mirror v Tie Case Sir E 1120 JFH
1025—   Soap box v Tie case Sir E 1110 JFH 1055—   Collar
box v Tie case Sir E = total 1150 JFH = total 1195 JFH wins

a night

6 March 1916— curious dreams last night had by several tent-mates probably the effects of yesterday's greasy feast my dream takes shape in endeavouring to drown multi-coloured hounds of dachshund (German sausage) breed my efforts not fraught with success for the dachshunds after assuming the form of seals eye me complacently with grinning eyes & the gargoyle grimaces of "Billikens" then so burning are our desires for liberation we more or less dream sailing free in luxuriant comfort of our ocean liner our dreams also take that incubus form where we gather at grand festival & as we commence eating the food fades from our eyes leaving our hunger un-appeased

a day

13 March 1916— never has time seemed to drag so much as to-day windy (SW) & foggy & the atmosphere very depressing even a desert isle would be more acceptable to this drifting imprisonment of mental & physical inertia & anxiety is felt by all that it is time to be making a move we seem to be in an icy maze when the ice does open a dense fog obscures everything for 50 yards & when it clears the temperature falls rapidly & freezing immediately sets in we only await open water then a fond fare-well to "Drifting Patience Camp"

a note

about provisions—   Paraffin 36 gallons
Sledging ration 24 cases HP biscuits 12
boxes Nut food 13 cases (1300 rations)
Sugar 2 lumps daily Trumilk 2 cases Salt
400 ¾ ounce pckts Dog pemmican 114
cakes Fuel in hand 21 days Kerosine &
Benzine ¾ gallon per day viz approx. 56
days Proposed blubber approx. 50 days?
= TOTAL 127 days

a day

30 March 1916— a huge sea leopard secured during morning enables us to increase daily meat ration an essential expedient to preserve strength of all & in the leopard's stomach some 50 pre-digested fish in excellent condition their own stomachs in turn crammed full with amphipods the fish reserved for to-morrow's breakfast remainder of dogs shot & skinned a few steaks cut off the young dogs fried & prove exquisitely tender & flavorous especially Nelson who equalled veal some amusement during the cooking the dog drivers standing around blubber stove with airs of proprietorship cajoling Cook to give special attention to the esculent fillets of their one time favourite as the steaks frizzle away Crean admonishes Cook for allowing Nelson to mix with Gruss & then Macklin complains that Gruss is being ruined by scorching a casual observer might think the explorer in some measure cold hearted especially if he notices mouths a-watering where tears ought to be expected but hunger levels us all to that of the other species & our saying that "sledge dogs are born for work & bred for food" merely the sum rationale of experience

a month

March 1916— gloomy day cold in tent— play cards
while-away rest of time discussing "the wind"— hands
numb with cold— our palates are depraved our food
almost entirely indigenous meats of the floe our capacity
for fats insatiable what then must we smell like? seals
no doubt— rime crystals veneer all things beautiful
with miniature fern like forms— finish "Vandover &
the Brute" by Norris— begin reading Ian Hamilton—
weary day spent sewing— I find another use for seals
viz their blubber possesses magic solvent properties on
dirt accumulated on playing cards— feeling weary—
dawn 4AM— feed ourselves imaginary feasts to be
indulged on our return— reading "20 Years After" by
Dumas living on one's imagination the only way to pass
time— rations cut to ½ sufficient to keep one healthy
& in constant hunger— slowly nibbling meal of one 2
oz biscuit & three lumps sugar provides mental effect of
a satisfying repast— wrap up 1lb tin of dog pemmican
in sock & take into sleeping-bag so by morning it may be
tolerably thawed— hand so numb it is difficult to write

a night

1 April 1916— sleep-less night beset by blizzard & floe breaking
up at 8PM all hands alarmed by night-watch a crack developing in
dangerous proximity to camp subsequent investigation exhibits a
split bifurcating floe & separating sledges from the tents the crack
after remarkable dodging of tents passes under sledge runners as if
possessed of devilish intelligence & the sledges & meat pile quickly
transferred to safety we return to tents fully equipped & ready for
a recurrence while through-out night the fractured floes impelled by
wind & actuated by sea-swell maintain a continual bumping that sets
one's heart leaping vague forebodings of camp being split into bits
by morning

a snap

of liberty!— 8AM an immense field of pack-ice comes drifting down upon us surrounding floe & preventing escape to open water— from adjacent hummock heaving like a vessel at sea one has a transcending view of an infinity of ice covered ocean-berg fragments shattered floes & brash ice grinding crunching groaning into indescribable chaos under the mighty influence of Cape Horn rollers— we view this profound menace & when it seems our floe must SPLIT under the rolling motion the ice opens up magically the boats loaded & launched & finally we are FREE!

a day

12 April 1916—   two days wind from NE we anticipate
50 miles further to West after breakfast boats get away 8
AM beautiful Sunshiny morning the pack radiant with pink
flush of Sun-rise & resembling ruins of Empyrean marble
cities with fair NW wind the James Caird Dudley Docker
& Stancombe Wills making SW course their object being
King George Island we pass fields of old fragmentary pack
on which bask great numbers of seals at evening we scout
about for a floe to which we may anchor several attempts
made til the Dudley Docker moored by a long painter to a
hummock the painter of Stancombe Wills then fastened to
her stern & the James Caird finally taking up the rear until
9PM we are beset by drift ice threatening every minute to
crush the boats this new enemy staved off with boat hooks
& oars the wind changing to SW we begin to drive back on
to floe & anchoring line is immediately severed the rest of
night spent drifting in sea of loose brash & newly formed
pan-cakes the boats to keep with one another stay tethered
together

a night

13 April 1916— I am mildly superstitious of numbers & this day
almost makes an end to us all   during morning the heavily laden
boats run under sail with a fair SE wind developing into a half gale
by noon   the boats are driven before it & forced into open ocean
then as night draws on with increasing seas Sir E calls to "heave to"
a sea anchor hastily constructed from the Dudley Docker's oars &
the boats tethered in line   through-out night all three continually
ship seas that break over & freeze thereon the ice must be chipped
away hourly   owing to treacherous cross currents the boats refuse
to lie true to their moorings but constantly bring up on each other
& needs must be staved off with hooks   then trial upon trial our
ejection into the sea is so rapid we are unable to take on any ice &
all being in sore need of water our wet condition & the agonizing
cold plus the need of sleep makes life well nigh unbearable   never
was dawn more anxiously awaited never did a night seem so long

a day

14 April 1916— welcome dawn! & with it something even more
welcome a glimpse of land! Clarence & Elephant Islands directly a-
head some 30 miles what a contrast to the terrors of the night the
Sun rising calm from pink mists over the "promised land" tipping
a peak til it becomes a vast gilt pyramid we take to rowing watch it
slowly loom closer assume finite detail 3PM 10 miles from shore &
no further headway this disheartening circumstance caused by tidal
current & as evening draws on the wind increases to gale raising a
big cross-sea & taxing our exhausted capacities the waters rake the
boats & spindrift hurls & strikes one's face like a whip we lose sight
of the Wills several times thinking she has foundered when all of a
sudden she emerges on a white crest from the blackness of the sea
I am fascinated by this wild scene & exult in our mastery over such
savage elemental display

a day

15 April 1916—— we coast leisurely along phantom like in the dim misty light of dawn until light sufficiently advanced for safe navigation much gratification caused by running into glacier ice some of which is hauled aboard & eaten with avidity to quench our burning thirsts at Cape Valentine a small sheltered beach is observed & landing conducted expeditiously & without accident the boats being hauled above high water onto the shingly beach conceive our joy on setting foot on solid earth after 170 days of life on a drifting floe each day filled with anxiety & being driven whither? it is sublime having trod but heaving decks & transient ice & one may finally feel one is walking on "reality" not subject to drift & gaping caprices that maroon & drop one into the sea

a snap

of land— landing effected in the eve of time for so many
of party emaciated by exhaustion & exposure they could not
have survived another 12 hours— Blackborrow is carried
from boat both feet frostbit some dozen cases of hands toes
in like condition— many suffer from temporary aberration
walking aimlessly about others shivering as with palsy— a
number of seals basking on beach perfunctorily stripped of
blubber & after partaking of steaks & draught of Trumilk all
turn in almost instantly deep in slumber— how delicious
to wake to a penguin's chanting croaks mingling with music
of the sea to fall asleep & wake again— to feel this is real
& we have reached LAND

a vista

of Elephant Island— cliffs throw serrated scarps
a thousand feet into the skies— glaciers tumble in
crevassed cascades down to the sea— occasional
glimpses of an ice clad interior beneath white peaks
looming four to five thousand feet & rarely visible
for clouds— wind storm & snow incessant while
willy willy eddies striking down gorges like bursting
tornadoes lash sea into spindrift & wrath— when
the Sun pierces clouds & mists the peaks & sea are
glorified with transcending gradations of shade &
light how I miss my camera & Cinematograph then

a note

about the Caird— preparations in active progress for
relief journey to South Georgia the carpenter makes a
start decking out Caird & hopes to have her finished by
22nd provisioning includes boat rations & stores for 6
men for 1 month plus 8 galls Petroleum 1 tin Spirit 30
boxes Matches 10 boxs Flamers 1 box Blue Lights 2
Primus stoves & parts & frickers 1 Cooker complete 6
Sleeping-bags Binoculars Sextant Compass Candles Oil
Charts Needle & twine Sea anchor Fishing line Aneroid
Boathook spare clothes sox etc a bit of blubber for bait
the Caird nearing completion requiring but canvassing I
spend most of to-day in private consultation with Sir E
the James Caird now complete & God willing leaves to-
morrow Wild left in charge of Elephant Isle the ringed
penguins from rookery near our camp having had quite
enough of weather congregate en masse on beach then
migrate during morning lucky birds! o! to be a penguin

a day

24 April 1916—   mid-day the Caird hoists her sail to
three ringing cheers & so commences one of the most
hazardous arduous voyages ever attempted in a small
boat great confidence is reposed in her crew Sir E Capt
Worsley Tom Crean & three sailors proven veterans &
seasoned by salt & experience 700 miles the distance to
South Georgia 700 miles of wintry seas the Caird is an
excellent vessel & guided by "providence" should make
Leith Harbour in 14 days it is intended to commission
the Undine of Grytviken Whaling Coy to rescue party
how we shall count the days

a note

21 April 1916—   to whom this may concern viz executors
assigns etc under is my signature to the following instructions
in the event of my not surviving the boat journey onto South
Georgia I here instruct Frank Hurley to take complete charge
& responsibility for exploitation of all films & photographic
reproductions of each negative taken on this Expedition the
aforesaid films & negatives to become the property of Frank
Hurley after due exploitation in which the moneys paid to my
executors will be according to the contract made at the start
of the Expedition the exploitation expiring after a lapse of 18
months from date of first public display I bequeath binoculars
to Frank Hurley EH SHACKLETON witness John Vincent

a month

April 1916— explosive punctuations of schools of whales— No 5
tent torn to shreds— observe whales fulmars petrels seals & secure
large Weddell in calf— atrocious weather wet drifting snow— we
retire to bags which are saturated with water at 5PM to steam & fug for
14 hours— sleeping gear & apparel ooze water— magnificent night
moon-light silvering sea with mystic charm the frowning coast standing
in dense silhouette against a star spangled sky— blowing Adelie Land
blizzard with pea soup drift— all work suspended & party sheltering
in tents which threaten momentarily to collapse— weather atrocious
mist snow wet— Hudson laid up in tent with badly frostbit hands &
suffering mental break-down the results of exposure in boat— a sea
elephant secured— most wretched weather conceivable it raining all
night nearly washed out of tents— roof rains water one might just as
well sleep in the open— gloomy seas breaking over dull white bergs
& sinister coast— everything sodden— blizzard all day— I miss
Sir Ernest admirable tent mate with whom time flew by over cigarette
& discourse— expect relief in about a fort-night— spend all day in
tent

a note

about our camp—   the size of ground space enclosed
18 ft x 12 ft the roof formed by two over-turned boats
resting on two low walls covered in canvas   the small
blubber bogie installed radiates pleasant warmth allows
cooking & fills the place with smoke & soot so much
our eyes run & our lungs nigh choke   the entire party
of 22 sleep in this space snugly though sardiniously with
stretchers arranged between the thwarts   6 of the lucky
squeeze into each boat the remainder unlucky on floor

a vista

of our camp— the highest point of spit Cape Wild is a
narrow neck jutting out from main-land some 350 yards it
joins main-land at base of magnificent spine shaped peak
the ocean termination a precipitous rocky bluff about 120
feet in height guarded oceanwise by inlet presenting a flat
jagged face called the Gnomon— to the East the coast
stretching in glorious vistas of perpendicular peaks end at
exquisitely cast Cornwallis Island all capped with glaciers
cascading like frozen cataracts— & West-ward another
gorgeous blue glacier debouching SW blizzards incessant
avalanches— a distant view is hidden though one does
glimpse isolated islets known as Seal Rocks— from my
elevated look-out a view beautiful beyond imagination yet
unwelcome over an ocean obscured by pack-ice the faint
miraged line observed yesterday having resolved into one
vast impenetrable field— there is a fine gravelly beach
on which we secure penguins & seals such is our home &
environment— given camera & plates one could spend
a year in Aesthetic contentment

a day

4 May 1916— the Sun hath risen! welcome Old
Jamaica! we greet thy genial face that makes all of
Nature smile & warms our hearts to happiness &
joy his rays shine on you & you feel that thrill of
existence the throb of life you stand entranced by
his sublime display & feel the bliss of being alive
soon the rosy tints turn a shimmering effulgence
thus heralding the birth of another day autumn's
days are short-lived for the Sun after describing
his 8 hour arc in the Heavens goes to rest in the
ocean in a blaze of golden glory the landscape in
sympathetic harmony assumes once more a flamy
tinge & then like dying embers of a fire takes on
that cold ashen tint of evening & stars rush out &
fill the sky like silver spangles the waters lap lazily
& Nature rests

a snap

of my comrades— the sparkling eyes & glint on aluminium
mugs the stream of flickering light thrown out the open bogie
door making weird dancing shadows on the insides of boats
makes me think of a council of brigands holding revelry after
escape from a chimney or coalmine— blubbery emanations
& odours from 22 crowded "seven month un-washeds" plus
blue tobacco smoke productive of an atmosphere distinctly
unsavoury— conversation after evening Hoosh wanders to
civilization to what we intend doing to eating to doing things
not likely to be done— after "smoke O" the tenants of attic
bunks swing into repose with monk like agility & the "ground
plan" spread with sleeping-bags into which owners retreat like
gigantic snails— the blubber night light sheds a feeble glow
over this catacomb like scene of objects resembling mummies
these objects are us

a note

about food—   small batches of Gentoo penguins
come ashore about 30 secured their stomachs filled
with euphausia also one seal the latter a gratifying
addition to blubber store all hands kill & skin over
35 penguins we indulge in snaring paddies of which
there are great numbers caught during day & to be
tried for lunch to-morrow find new Hoosh recipe
viz 3 disbanded penguin carcasses chopped up then
simmered in 2 galls water the results accepted with
general approval for lunch we have paddies caught
yesterday the birds all plump & fat & when fried in
blubber taste like veal the equal of any I have eaten
the birds caught by spreading slip noose near some
bait & being greedy they walk right in & voila! the
"meal beau ideal"

a month

May 1916—   dull weather wet Scotch mist—   great numbers
snow petrels & Dominican gulls in bay—   wretched day the
blowing about of ice sheets the size of window panes all kept
indoors—   winter is hard upon us the spit & gravel beach now
hidden beneath a deep layer of ice while reefs & outlying rocks
wear ice caps of frozen sea spray—   Wild "do you like dough
nuts?" McIlroy "rather" Wild "damn easily made too I like them
cold with a little jam"—   secure 25 Gentoos & 7 sheatbills—
excellent lunch of parboiled peas fried in blubber alas! we regret
they are our last—   another day in Nature's art gallery the sea
a liquid mirror canopied by a sky almost blue black—   monthly
issue of matches to smokers 18 matches each—   sit in murky
atmosphere talking of things already spoken of a hundred times
before—   cold raw day—   no birds or seals—   installing our
selves for the winter little hope being entertained of immediate
relief—   spend day talking motors & designing intended 35 ft
auxiliary cruiser—   spend day improvising Antarctic alphabet—
now a month since the James Caird's departure—   sleeping 15
hours on end—   no duties—   right glad to see the last of May

a day

22 June 1916—   mid-winter's day Sun-rise 920AM 5½ hours Sun-light
temp 30 Sun not observable owing to dense sea fog ice free ocean with
light surf rolling in day of festivities extra rations issued <u>Breakfast</u> full
strength sledging ration <u>Lunch</u> "pudding" made from mouldy nut food
bars 20 biscuits 4 sledging rations boiled together <u>Tea</u> Hoosh of cut up
penguin legs livers hearts & 4 sledging rations <u>Toasts</u> the King the Sun's
return the Boss & crew of the Caird sweet-hearts & wives the evening
passes convivially & pleasantly with a concert no paucity of talent some
30 items being rendered 50% of which are topical songs & recitations
owing to lack of room Artists perform items from well within sleeping-
bags turn in 10PM & sleep well except for stertorous snoring of Lees
whom I kick on the head many times & pelt with pebbles off the floor

a month

June 1916— 606 Gentoos secured since landing 17th April— food eaten out of mugs by fingers as knives forks etc lost during escape in boats— penguin feathers reindeer hairs from moulting sleeping-bags find way into food but go unheeded— heated argument indulged in over encroachment of an inch in space has been going on for the past half hour— all hands assemble on strand awaiting penguins— all meals being cooked at one firing due to fuel economy the evening meal being the vilest tasting mixture— a successful experiment with new drink 3% absolute alcohol (for Primus stove) sweetened with sugar this we hold secret for mid-winter's day— surprise & secure magnificent Weddell bull the equivalent of 80 penguins— clear mild day— time passing wearily nothing to do but sleep eat wait— despicably snowy & wet— this indolent life & enervating climate clearly responsible for mental / physical coma— pleasure found in watching ice blocks bob around in surf— large number of Gentoos forthwith captured we let none escape— Blackborrow's left foot to be operated on to-day his frostbit toes to be amputated— 9 weeks since the departure of Caird — a sea elephant pup secured severely scarred— tobacco run short some awesome substitutes concocted of a quality I can-not speak but EUREKA! what aromas! penguin feathers rope sennegrass dried meat & numerous etceteras sampled to satiate craving for tranquillizer "My Lady Nicotine"— 81 Gentoo penguins captured to-day making 524 <u>total</u> for month

a night

2 July 1916—   usual Saturday evening toast
to sweet-hearts & wives & Sir E & crew of the
Caird I invent new beverage ingredients Spirit
Vinii meth hot water sugar a pinch of nutmeg
(the latter carried in mistake for tin of pepper)
first sip giving impression of hot peppermint
second gulped with "bated breath" noses held
& faces awry recalling "Vermifuge" the after-
effects while producing a "mild glow" leaving
one's palette dry with flavour of match-heads

a snap

of an interior—   now that "Wild's Window"
allows a shaft of day-light to dimly illuminate
our interior I make note of what can be seen
from my corner—   this little window which
is sewn into the wall contiguous to my claim
& affords much pleasure measures only 6 ins
x 6 ins & originally the lid of chronometer—
on very rare occasions the early Sun bids us
good morning & sheds a beam of welcome
yet rather misplaced effulgence on the grimy
features of Cook bending over frying pots &
"hash up"—   more frequent blizzard days
this little window frosts over & a diversity of
exquisite palm leaf crystal forms appear even
then it transmits sufficient lighting to read by

a night

26 July 1916—   a little zest lent to the monotony of
our immutable existence last night when turning over
in sleeping-bag my hand plunges into WATER which
induces dream of falling through cracked floes into the
sea I awake with apprehension the reassuring grunting
of miscellaneous snorers dispelling my fears til further
investigations reveal "floors awash" viz yesterday's rain
having drained into sleeping space which is now lower
than exterior surface the latter having built up by snow
increments nothing to do but awaken Wild & he James
McIlroy & self begin mid-night bail some sixty galls of
evil smelling liquid

a day

30 July 1916—   to-day seems particularly monotonous
& the wild magnificence of the cliffs which limit us to the
circumscribed confines of "Cape Wild" loom through mist
like prison walls ominous & inaccessible if there were only
some duties useful or otherwise the burden of time might
feel more pleasant but a gloomy day the very embodiment
of dreary inhospitality our sole exercise to promenade up
& down the 80 yards of spit or climb "Look-out Bluff" to
scan sky-line for a mast one grows fatigued of continually
estimating days from Caird's departure to hoped for sight
of relief

a month

July 1916— nothing doing— pleasant calm day though dull—
no penguins— reading Kane's "Grinnel Expedition in Search of
Sir John Franklin"— a Weddell seal drifts by on pack— a very
noticeable lengthening of day-light discernible— altitude of moon
about 50° illumines sea with day-light brilliancy— promenade spit
in moon¬-light such transcending conditions ideal for honey-moon
couples— successful experiment "Fried Penguin Legs" a distinct
improvement over boiling which extracts all juices leaving leathery
synthetic rubber like meat firmly attached by stringy sinews to the
bone— observe single rainbow the first I have seen for over two
years— pass time with snare but birds extremely wary— spend
to-day contemplating gorgeous colouring & jagged glacier cliffs—
finish Kane 1st Vol— commence "Nordenskjold"— fusillade
of flying ice clattering on tent roof resembles a miniature shrapnel
bombardment— cricket during afternoon the bat a small piece
of sledge runner the balls pebbles from strand we are sadly out of
practice— 9 months since ship's crushing— nothing happens

a day

1 August 1916— two years since the Endurance left London
& one since she experienced her first severe nipping from the
pressure what vicissitudes & trials we have passed through what
days of incessant anxiety til she was finally crushed 2½ months
later & then our weary watching & waiting on the floe drifting
North-ward to where? six months of this well nigh intolerable
life of insecurity the final disruption of ice & our phenomenal
escape to our present habitat flit through the mind as a chaotic
confused night-mare though we have been dwelling here nearly
4 months this latter period seems longer than preceding balance
of the year surely the Aurora will come this month I have been
reading "Nordenskjold" to-day & so similar to our own position
is his narrative that I actually feel it is OUR party being rescued
by the Uruguay

a month

August 1916—   absolutely nothing doing but waiting all keep indoors
owing to miserable weather—   sitting like an invalid in one's sleeping-
bag re-reading the same few books—   Sun-light gives ineffable charm
to the mountains over which thin wisps of cloud drift with a variety of
chiaroscuro effects—   30 Gentoos secured—   what an idle use-less
existence—   I try fishing again but no luck—   nothing of any import
beyond drying my sleeping-bag which got very wet from leaking rain in
night—   we are heartily sick of being compelled to kill every bird that
comes ashore for food & will be pleased when the sea elephants return
one bull would equal at least 150 penguins—   Wild shoots a leopard it
escapes—   one little penguin falls into soot & soils his white breast he
appears as concerned as a dignified old gentleman who has dirtied his
expensive dress suit—   I discover that dulse when boiled assumes jelly
like consistency & if sugared tastes like arrowroot—   a large Weddell
comes ashore & is captured she contains a well developed foetis—   a
discussion with James concerning radio activity—   read "King Henry
V"—   wretched weather again—   nought to do but stay in one's bag
or wander the snow

a day

30 August 1916— <u>day of wonders</u> whilst party at lunch
Marston & I without shelling limpids when I call him to a
curious piece of ice on horizon with striking resemblance
to a SHIP at the same time *a ship! rounds the Gnoman Island*
we immediately call "Ship O!" which is instantly followed
by general exodus of cheering the Hoosh left to burn the
meal forgotten a beacon kindled & attention attracted to
which ship signals response she comes within distance &
lowers a boat & we recognise the BOSS & thank God for
his safety! all gear hurriedly rowed to Yelcho in just under
an hour we subsequently learn it is FOURTH attempt to
effect our rescue! that night a musical evening & we hear
all the news of the war of the world etc etc etc <u>AT LAST!</u>

a day

31 August 1916—   I am not so susceptible to emotions but
this happy reunion with our comrades whom we had almost
given up for lost & our happy release with these lonely peaks
like mute sentinels witnessing our departure has left indelible
feelings two boat-loads suffice to carry all worldly belongings
& selves on board & 2PM we are underway engines at speed
racing for the open seas & freedom o! the bliss of feeling the
motion of the sea the music of fresh though foreign voices &
to sense at last our anxieties & privations are ended & we will
soon be re-united with home & civilization yet as those noble
peaks fade into mist I can scarce repress sadness to leave this
land that has rained on us its bounty & has for so long been
our salvation

a vista

of BLISS—   our first thoughts are to wash *this novel sensation*
rejuvenating & giving us something of the appearance of our
fellows—   then soup Irish stew & peaches how joyfully our
palates respond to these new flavours—   & coffee! & wine!
we toast old Bacchus the King the Boss the James Caird the
Chilian Government the Chilian Navy Captain Pardo etc etc
which toasting only ceases on the "expiry" of available vintage
—   the excitement of the night does not enable sleep—   I
lie on the floor wrapped in a blanket & thinking how ineffably
pleasing to be kept awake by the throb of engines hurrying us
back to life than lie like smouldering logs on Elephant Isle—
there is so much to hear of the wonderful adventures of our
Boss his companions on the Caird & of their crossing those
blizzard swept ranges of South Georgia & three unsuccessful
attempts to free us from the besetting ice good old Boss!—
multifarious magazines & cablegrams provide a profusion of
data that acquaint us with the world to which we have all been
strangers

a day

3 September 1916— beautiful Sun-rise with fine mist effect over
hills & mountains surrounding Punta Arenas it is a charming scene
clad with foliage extremely inviting to us who have not gazed on a
blade of grass for two years the Yelcho bedecked with flags moves
off from her moorings & everywhere the Chilian Ensign welcomes
on nearing the jetty we are deafened by tooting whistles & cheering
motor craft on landing we are greeted by immense crowd & Naval
Band as we march through town in filthy Elephant Island togs not
ever have I imagined such a warm reception could be given to utter
strangers such a crowd never witnessed in Punta Arenas 8000 9000
must be gathered & if each man were a brother kindlier feelings or
sentiments could not be expressed at 9PM a British Club dinner in
our honour songs sung speeches made Expedition men dance with
Club men & the halls resounding with continuous bursts of genuine
laughter when one is amongst those men having actually subscribed
to equip the ship which has so determinedly attempted to rescue us
he is with the right sort of friends

THE PICTURE SHOW TOUR

December 1919–January 1920

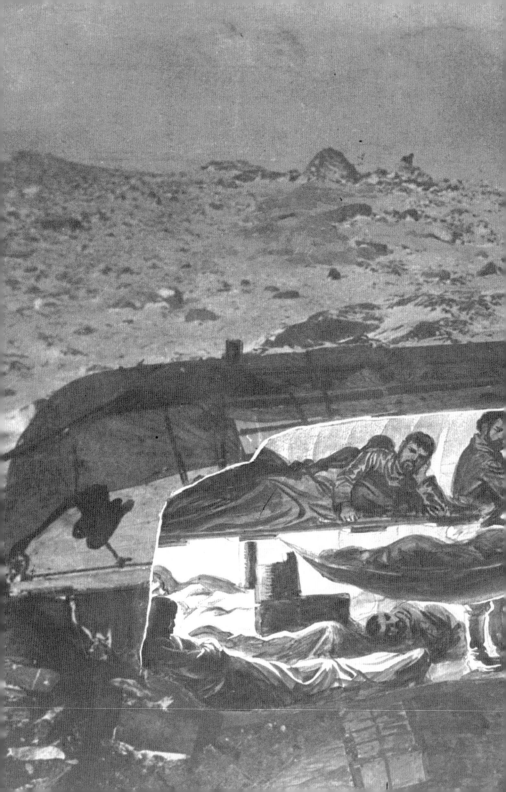

premiere

6th Dec 1919 we open at "Kings Cross" first day a distinct success— *we steam from Grytviken Whaling Station on 5th December 1914 after bidding adieu to good friends—* begin Season at "Pav" this evening to full House first day a distinct success— *MacDougall can be seen the last figure waving Bon Voyage! til we round Mount Dusie & head for open sea & the South—* commence Season at "Strand" sessions being 11AM 3PM 8PM I speak evening & matinees Wednesday & Saty first day a distinct success— *I observe Sun rising from behind a berg & day breaks with the glory & charm of an Empyrean dawn*

cast

morning into town & complete final arrangements for Tour I am to be accompanied by Terry O'Shea operator & William Mazengarb assist ~~operator~~ lecturer the latter will follow on to-morrow— *during evening Wordie Clark James & self repair to cabin to partake of Scotch Hogmaney Cake brought from home by Wordie—* spend afternoon studying the types of Sydney beauty which so far I have not confirmed existence of— *have arrived at that limit of negroid discoloration from smoking bogie & blubber lamps at least comforting to feel we can become no filthier—* Brisbanians a weary looking lot minus dash & energy & the women do not suffer from good looks to any noticeable extent— *crew with few exceptions a very meagre set ignorant & illiterate & of far more complaining disposition than Scientific staff—* Adelaide for Culture I don't think!— *regretable to state that many conduct themselves in manner unworthy of British sailors they are grossly incapable of discoursing on even the most commonplace subjects—* class of people attracted are all that could be desired it is a pleasure to speak to them— *impossible to write coherently on account of the harangueing going on—* with a sigh of relief I fall into the lap of Morpheus & dream of new scenarios & squashy romantic films to suit this quixotic mob

venue

Sydney performance given to packed House over 2200 filling seats &
stairs & standing in these big theatres crammed with all classes one does
not hear a sound all seems b-r-e-a-t-h-l-e-s-s it is great— *all sit on floor
with feet jammed against lathes to prevent sliding & looking like a music hall gallery
in Topsy Turveydom*— Brisbane "Olympia" a filthy ill kept dirty dusty
House & LAST place in world to go in decent suit of clothes— *peering
down one of these man traps we look into black nothingness*— one's words
chase each other around & hurl themselves back in confused jargon &
the HEAT! the theatres more crammed & hotter than Hades! thank
Heavens I am showing ICE pictures & even they thaw on screen— *ice
closed but reopening this evening*— from Aristocratic heights of "Town Hall"
descend into dungeon confines of "Britannia" a mediocre crowd chiefly
Servant girls & squawking kids the table from which one spouts erected
20 feet from picture & one feels more like a babbling auctioneer than
Dignified Orator— *menial discontent in the fo'c'sle*— Adelaide "Pavillion"
continuous show with 1200 capacity the House packs early & hundreds
turned away ventilation totally inadequate & instead of large sliding roofs
there seems great anxiety to keep hot air IN— *in striking contrast to Adelie
Land where fiendish blizzards rage incessantly there seems something uncanny about
this place if I had my choice I scarcely know which I would select*— cabletrams
clang & Luna Park switchback fills House with continuous din—
*immense blocks of ice piled in a ruin like chaos the din like distant artillery boom
boom*

apparatus

I am appreciative of my operators' efforts & excellent results achieved
with makeshift apparatus— *engage in fixing up three 20 foot poles with
bamboo spreaders to carry four wires for wire-less*— slide lantern gives me
qualms as lens held in by sticky tape & I have frequent apprehensions of

it falling out— *rig Cinema on sledge & film Macklin's team following in my wake the combination of movement should prove unique effect*— O'Shea & self make early start at "Olympia" fixing up buzzer control from footlights to operating box the box made of galvanized iron & installed with two primaeval machines needs must be re-wired— *find blubber excellent flux for soldering*— spend morning hunting up lenses visit Bonds & Kodaks where I have trouble getting away for their tongues & questions are many— *Hudson & self make another attempt to receive wire-less signals but as it is bright day-light all night efficiency of receiver is marred*— continued trouble securing lenses at present Cinema picture much larger than slide projection but hope to correct this to-morrow— *construct small window from 9 x 7 piece of celluloid rescued from photo portfolio & sew it on to Hut "wall"*— eventually secure lenses & find them to suit admirably but the best laid schemes of enthusiasts gang off to die & new arrangement of optics nearly ends in destruction of slides— *a spar rigged with heavy ice chisel to be operated as reciprocating drill*— a hitch in projection this evening the picture thrown upon screen very poorly the light fluctuating badly this I attribute to my operator very much the worse for festive Season I threaten to send him back to Sydney & have quite disillusioned him as to his indispensability— *owing to heavy rime dispositions on wire-less poles & rigging it is deemed advisable to take them down*— mitigate decision to send O'Shea back to Sydney & after hearty reprimand make him promise to drink only water in future

scenery

cross into Queensland 910AM country drought stricken in pitiable state— *frost smoke rising from water tinged red by Sun-set giving appearance of fires in every direction*— find scenery merchant hard at work converting portico into ice berg while over all waxes & wanes the aurora I think the Artist must have had very strong attack of hallucinations & drained "many a draught" his interpretation of an aurora eloquent of the fiery squirms that haunt the brain of a Delirium Tremens— *Sun extending to horizon & 15° above it an intense pillar of light*— morning sightseeing not of course that there is anything to see— *striking recurrence of parhelia exceeding in brilliancy & colour all previously witnessed the atmosphere highly charged with scintillating rime crystals which show modifications of the hexagon*— a great paucity of trees & gardens in the suburbs & private homes— *colours thrown up on clouds as though ocean ablaze the Sun's orb sinking into sea like a golden ball such effect one would expect in the desert but this is a land of varied & magic atmospheres an Artist's paradise*— a plague of beetles have done much harm to our roses— *the wind is rising & playing mischievous pranks generally*— not a tuft of grass to be seen even the leaves of the hardy old Gum trees dry & parched— *the prospect one might liken to a glimpse of ice fields on the moon beautiful in grandeur beyond conception*— once more aboard train I find interest in the Riverina where the wheat has been gathered & the hill-sides like sandhills golden with stubble— *observe large areas diatomaceous coloured ice with pools of honeycomb*— everything exquisitely verdant the tips of Gums waving tender red shoots in a Eucalyptus breeze— *remarkable reappearance of Sun at noon to-day when it rises/disappears/rises again*— fields covered with ricks & sheaves— *during evening a fine double halo around moon with mock moons*— the day's heat has subsided & the setting Sun lit with strong sidelight— *magnificent Sun-set tipping snow clad peaks with delicate alpengluehn & Sirius on horizon gleams a distant beacon*

audience

the story which all seem to say is unique & thrilling received magnificently it is some reward speaking to two thousand up-turned faces all eager interested intent— *large numbers of ringed penguins follow the ship's wake*— a more enthusiastic audience I could not have spoken to during afternoon they clap & cheer wildly— *about noon two snow petrels hover around camp & settle on snow a few yards away*— evening crowd absolutely un-responsive until the end when applause is great— *large mobs of Adelies scatter over floe their plaintive croaks heard everywhere—* I look at the crowded Houses & can-not help thinking the audience are warriors to cram themselves into a theatre hot as an oven— *ice 200 yards astern cracks & four emperor penguins emerge therefrom—* poor House the most apathetic & phlegmatic crowd they are as cold as the frozen pictures I show them why I don't know because temperature of theatre is high about 100 Degrees I would far rather speak to an empty House filled with logs of wood— *two killer whales poke their heads out of water & gaze at us admiringly—* the sociology of crowds gives one food for thought & I intend scientifically investigating the problem this evening I repeat precisely same words project precisely same pictures am even more forceful in Rhetoric & yet last night's audience on a crest of enthusiasm & to-night a trough of apathy— *noticeable paucity of animal life—* what to me is paradoxical is that heat produces a cold audience & so this evening the House suffers heat & I get the "shivers"— *a number of Antarctic terns attracted to our camp fill the air with sweet jargoning—* an unsympathetic mob about as emotional as a crowd of sea elephants occasionally there is isolated applause but I think it more for exercise or to make a disturbance than anything else

narrative

thank Heavens man is an adaptable brute— *amidst profound & over-whelming forces we are absolute embodiment of help-less futility What Ho!—* with daybreak observe pleasant change in country the very antithesis of burnt up herbage of the North here are green trees & grasses & water & fat cattle a park-land to a desert— *gratifying to feel we are only 80 miles from Vasel Bucht however a disquieting possibility of us freezing in & becoming part of the floes—* man is essentially a discontented animal I hear rumours of tea being too strong puddings too sweet what hardships we (don't) have to endure— *we are now anchored to the ice—* evening the Union Theatre's publicity "bug" carries me off to the 'Mail' office where I needs must give column of my wretched experiences which just now are becoming a bug-bear— *all hope not given up of breaking free yet to be on safe side now beginning to accumulate stock of seal meat for winter*— the hills are golden with ungathered grain & the evening mists blurring the distant hills make the landscape one of ineffable charm "wow wow"— *this morning in no mood to greet day with song for our floe has turned round during the night & with it the wind thank Heavens man is an adaptable brute*— & so I find my-self talking about Xmasses spent on ship & floe to a full House & carols be praised an appreciative one What Ho!— *New Year imbued with new hopes for the ice manifests most satisfactory aspect of breaking up since we entered it a year ago "wow wow"*— the picture story has stormed Brisbane & gripped the popular imagination as usual autographs the curse of "fame"— *it is hoped drift will dessiminate to enable communication to be effected with world outside*— my throat does not allow me indulging in elocutionary embellishments as it is tired after afternoon— *ship covered with sparkling snow like ground pearl shells the rigging tinselled with sifted diamonds & dogs & drivers alike feel the influence of such an exhilarating atmosphere*

season

morning to "Strand" to fit up appointments for coming Season— *count matches & find enough for twelve months supply very anxious however to reach Snow Hill early in Season to avoid wintering another year*— Season should be extended at least another week for while advertising at first fills House those who see picture spread the news & picture draws through sheer merit— *considering Season the ice has now reached critical point of disintegration*— Sydney & Melbourne do not as a rule experience such severe temperatures & comparatively small exodus from city scarcely reacts on the Houses— *through-out day a thaw sets in to-day everything between decks dripping & dogs very wet*— week at "Majestic" tremendous success every afternoon matinee & evening large numbers turned away— *what is the wind's direction is the breathword of the camp every puff or caprice given as much* *attention as if it were a delicate instrument—* the fruit Season has been splendid & growers have come into their own by receiving highest figure ever received— *it would appear ice has arrived at a dead-lock—* receive ~~Wire~~ letter from Musgrove stating they do not wish to exercise option to extend the Season ye gods be praised!

soliloquy I

the days pass wearily there is little to do & no-where to go when not lecturing at the "Strand"— *the monotony of slow progression I have relieved* *somewhat by printing series from negatives with intention of binding into pictorial log of* *Expedition—* after evening performance I meet old friend of Mawson Expedition George Ainsworth & find much enjoyment talking over Mawson affairs & happenings otherwise it is just a matter of talk/eat/sleep/loaf two of these only appeal to me— *morning exercise* *dogs & "dinkass" about generally then turn in at own desire after arduous day* *endeavouring to make time pass—* Queensland climate frightfully enervating & one can-not help but "go slow"— *hard to imagine we are drifting frozen* *& solid in the very heart of the Weddell Sea I often wonder what is to become of it* *all—* I do my best with futile results— *same morning jaunt no-game-no-life* *same exasperating patience to endure*

interlude

morning walk around Brisbane Gardens affords much pleasure— *all* *hands engage in game of Soccer on floe—* Mazengarb & self motor 26 miles out to Cleveland the village on ocean side & cool sea breezes Heavenly after swelter of town— *go for splendid ski run whilst others indulge in fierce* *game of Hockey with magnificent ski surface & breeze I speed as if possessed of* *wings—* morning to Adelaide Botanical Gardens much to my satisfaction they are exquisitely cared for & in my opinion superior to Sydney— *sledge race over "Khyber Pass" to ship with bets freely made on both sides chiefly in chocolate our Antarctic currency*— afternoon stroll around Wagga a well laid out country town boasting splendid shops & what delights greatly an avenue of trees— *McIlroy's dice affords much amusement all casting lots as to who will defer cost of taxis theatres dinners etc on returning home temperature −14.1*— pleasant drop in temperature & over-night downpour has made exhilarating the air the road-way winding ever up-ward through magnificent glades of Gums in perfect condition— *1 tin sardines being over we decide to cut cards for same & split contents into quarters McLeod Hussey Blackborrow & self lucky winners of two sardines each*— with Claude for motor run to neighbouring orchard which I enjoy to the full the plums & apricots just being picked— *"The Billabong" has atmosphere poetic to-night Macklin in bunk writing poetical verses & your humble doing the same*

refreshments

Mrs Hunter always has homely snack & big bumper of lemon squash ready on our return— *biscuits fried in blubber eaten with as much relish as though they were medicine*— lunched in Brisbane Gardens with Ainsworth & afternoon at hotel doing nothing— *four seals secured they are shot some two miles from ship & take us three hours to sledge them in*— after lunching at Cleveland & enjoying prospect & air return to Brisbane 530PM— *as we have no great surplus decision must be arrived at very soon as to whether to shoot the dogs*— lunch with Claude & mother at his home in Newtown— *Hoosh made of seal tongues seal livers seal brains flavoured with onion thickened with flour we are becoming true Gastronomists*— great fields of pineapples passed along the way— *penguin Omelette on an old tin plate*— Macclesfield is a quaint little village it might be Devon right down to the apple-trees Mrs Mott gives excellent lunch plentiful fresh & scrupulously served— *about 800 to 900 limpids collected a delicious change in diet eaten very s-l-o-w-l-y to derive maximum pleasure*— dine with Lockwoods at their charming home— *the meal is taken in silent gravity while crushing in progress & ominous sounds below*

accompaniment

afternoon to Brisbane Gardens the band blares & blares it reminds me of the Gippo Band in Cairo each instrument vieing to make itself predominant with neither execution nor melody— *lie in bunk listening to every note trying to imagine singer & song under civilized circumstances—* of course there has to be the invariable yelping babe which disturbs the quiet & interest of the thousand why folks bring infants in arms to such functions passes my comprehension completely this one & its mother ordered to quit— *numerous Adelie penguins amuse themselves following ship when Hussey playing a Scotch jig on banjo scares them off—* take evening run out to Henley Beach where Tramway band languidly performs the sea air refreshing but the music unemotional— *the pumps work faster & faster someone actually singing a "shanty" to their beat—* outside an organ drones & a parasite sings the sound filters into hall & discords with wails of half a dozen kids one just goes ahead like the Endurance heeding nothing grinding away at ice-pack— *from various cabins eminate efforts on violin mandolin banjo accordeon vieing for musical honours or rather dishonours—* I do my utmost to be heard by bellowing as loud as I can under such conditions one becomes a pure Automaton a mere mechanical Gramophone— *evening Gramophone concert at which all hands attend fo'c'sle included—* I envy orchestra for the noise they produce— *a few spoonfuls of methyl alcohol loosens the tongue of many a backward singer their voices accompanied by Hussey's banjo strangely out of place amidst profound silence of the floe*

lodgings

arrive Brisbane 640PM & to "Australian Hotel" a passable House with good table small rooms & no pretty waitresses or maids— *an unostentatious abode where one can study anatomy of ship's stout ribs to heart's content—* take up residence at the "Gresham" unpretentious & comfortable— *erect series of cabins in hold where ship's party will reside during winter the holders of these 6' 5" x 5' cubicles bestow various cognomens "The Anchorage" "Auld Reekie" "The Poison Cupboard" "The Knuts" "The Billabong"—* under great debt to hotel manageress a Mrs Hunter this generous soul has lost both sons at the Front & her motherly consideration has mitigated greatly the weariness of Tour— *to-day on arising from bunk which is immediately over Wordie's I step onto his face with stockinged foot & as stockings washed some three weeks previously he is awakened most effectually—* put up at "Scotts" in Melbourne a place where one pays for toothpicks & "swank"— *go below into old winter quarters & find water already well above floor the sound of splintering beams in darkness a little too imposing so I leave—* & so to rest tired & dream-less & at the tiresome hour of 5AM turn wearily from my inviting couch to the long journey Adelaide-wards— *remain in bunk most of time glancing out port-hole onto very dismal prospect & listening to homely crow like croak of penguins I ruminate on home & dear ones—* home to the two little Nips pictures of health & beautiful angels they have progressed well & make great joy over return of their dad it is good to be home again though it be for moments— *showers of reindeer hairs from bunk above mingle with dripping of thaw "but nevertheless I must confess by many & many a mile / this is the most palatial dwelling you'll find on Elephant Isle"*

management

prices charged at "Strand" positively ridiculous & could quite readily be doubled the management here lacks brains & foresight— *at mid-night cocoa & wishing Sir Ernest Many Happy Returns of 41st birthday—* must comment on kindly consideration of manager a Mr Reid— *Sir Ernest thoughtful as ever sledges out to meet us a mile from camp with cans of steaming tea personally I feel a Dr Johnson & could drain 36 cups—* Webb the manager regrets not running another week— *we keenly regret Sir E's announcement & must now await Nature's pleasure to free us—* manager is a quality of "stiff" & rough that looks more like a pub expeller— *Sir E ever on alert & as wise precaution has all sledging stores paraffin sledges sledging equipment stowed*

on deck in case of emergency such as ship being crushed— seats booked at 3/–
& 2/– & Union Theatres management do remarkably well— *one member*
places ice on Sir E's bogie mistaking it for coal & Sir E very irately wigs offender
(who also it is alleged put coal into ice pot)— manager whom I originally take
to be a "Yankee Stiff" not such a bad fellow after all he is none other
than "DIABLO" the man who used to perform the loop-the-loop stunt
on bicycle an ingenious being & has designed some quite clever
arrangements for theatre— *just now Boss making ready mustard plaster he*
having attack of the rheumatism— I suggest taking "Town Hall" for Saty
night the management very scared so I offer them £50 over expenses
however they still being unwilling I take "Town Hall" anyway & it is
crowded— *Sir E at present time dipping fingers into tin of Virol smoking*
Tabbard cigarettes reading epicures from Britannica— "Palais de Danse"
proprietors are as dissimilar as is possible except in money affairs
Solomons looks like a sea elephant that has swallowed a barrel & is just
about as apathetic Phillips is a needle a minnow they are both repulsive—
I especially admire Sir E he is one of the finest characters I have ever had the fortune
to meet

conveyance

leave Sydney 330PM by Brisbane Xpress our cases narrowly escape catching train
owing to faulty transport arrangements of Australasian Films— *delightful run*
with team during morning the faint day-light mingling with moon-light lending
a peculiar enchantment to frozen sea— day in train an ovenly ordeal the Sun
blazes & the drought stricken country throws back the heat intensely— *surface*
atrocious having to plug through soft snow into which we sink thigh deep— Per-
cy Correll takes us for extremely enjoyable motor run to Mount Lofty— *sur-*
face now disheartening with dogs sinking deep to bellies & having to practically
paddle their way— have a look at Correll's boat his intention of setting out to
Antarctic in this tub nothing short of SUICIDE Percy always the originator of
wild & fantastic schemes but this caps all I am striving to dissuade him from

such a RIDICULOUS & UNPROFITABLE undertaking— *perform variety of terpsichorean feats on ski to cross pressure ridge & brash filled leads*— return to Melbourne by ferry we call in at Port Arlington where human freight becomes rather tightly packed— *33 miles made last 24 hours slow progress due to dense packing of floes*— of course there has to be the inveterate hot axle so our arrival an hour overdue— *travel over extremely diversified packs hummocks ridges plains through which my good leader Shakespeare selects his own road with almost human intuition*— night in prehistoric sleeper that jolts & jars ones bones into disjointedness keeping one awake— *drive sledge out amongst hummocks ahead of ship after afternoon tea it being brilliantly moon-lit*— quarters on train far ahead of "Kennels" on Qsld & NSW lines so a tolerable rest & sleep something quite unusual

soliloquy II

am always hard put to it for originality— *am "home" again in Gartfern when suddenly brought to bearings by artillery of glacier debouching an avalanche into bay*— one becomes very rest-less on these peregrinations & I find it extremely difficult to concentrate one feels the impulse to be continually on the move— *I do not mind getting out & stretching legs although land over 300 miles away but prefer when temperature a little warmer it now being 53° below*— morning for stroll around docks the lure of the sea comes on strongly & as I tread the decks of these ocean greyhounds I long to be off with them— *owing to bad light am unable to discover track home & leave it to dogs to find their way back which they do*— evening lecture something to be endured & go through as speedily as possible— *although time hangs on one's hands it is impossible to concentrate one's thoughts in an icy maze & everything in a state of extreme compression*— it is with some feelings of relief when we draw away from Sydney— *a solitary Gentoo the only life visible & even he seems afraid*

finale

last night at Sydney— *the Sun departs to-day—* the Tour has been an arduous one & not without worry it has however been a phenomenal success— *Sir E hoists blue ensign at mizzen gaff to three lusty cheers & is last to leave—* & so the Brisbane Season comes to an end with record day & House— *pay final official visit to wreck with Boss & Wild yesterday's blizzard having put final touch to destruction—* whether it is gladness at the sight of relief ship which provokes such tremendous applause or knowledge it is the last slide I am uncertain about— *to ship's grave with Wild McIlroy & Marston salving numerous odds & ends ablated from snow & drift in which they were buried—* again whether it is my-self or the end of the story they applaud leaves me in some doubts— *our Hut will become a centre around which coveys of penguins will assemble to gaze & deliberate its origin—* audiences are cold [in]capable of comprehension until with a sigh of relief comes The End & one feels like the crowd he could clap himself that it is finally over

about the author

Jordie Albiston was born on the 30th of September, 1961, and grew up in Melbourne, Australia. She studied Literature and Women's Studies at Latrobe University, for which she received a PhD.

Including this title, she published fourteen poetry collections, three children's books and a handbook on poetic form. Two of her collections were adapted for musical theatre, both enjoying seasons at the Sydney Opera House. Albiston's work has been recognised by many awards, including the Mary Gilmore Award, the Wesley Michel Wright Prize and the NSW Premier's Prize. Albiston was honoured in 2019 with the Patrick White Literary Award and in 2022 (posthumously) received the John Bray Award in the Adelaide Festival Awards for Literature.

Albiston's work celebrated form and the notion of formal boundaries, whether traditional or experimental and self-imposed. She was the frequent creator of many otherwise unimagined poetic structures, including the various geometry-based forms that make up *Euclid's Dog*, and the fifteen-line sonnets from her award-winning book *Fifteeners*.

She has an entry in *Who's Who in Twentieth-Century World Poetry* and is mentioned in *The Cambridge Companion to Australian Literature* and *The Princeton Encyclopedia of Poetry & Poetics*.

Jordie Albiston died in Melbourne on the 28th of February, 2022, at the age of 60, leaving a husband and two children.

Jordie Albiston on documentary poetry and this volume

As a writer often working in the realm of documentary poetry, I've been challenged and rechallenged by a number of issues over the years. For example, nostalgia can be disruptive if you are merely looking to the past in order to confirm your own often false tenets of the present. I've found I must be particularly careful when approaching a subject that invokes a nostalgic response in me as this is when my own emotions can surreptitiously up-end the apple cart.

The concept of truth is perennially problematic, raising questions such as whose truth? Who has recorded this history and why? Is truth experienced differently according to who you are? Does truth transcend the usual divisions of class, gender and race? Is one person's truth another person's folly and so on? It certainly seems true to me that if history repeats itself it's because we repeat ourselves. Perhaps putting ourselves in another's position, walking a mile in another's shoes, will help us to apprehend and appreciate, learn, change, become better people, do less harm.

I've always been drawn to history as a source of material from which to create poems. My first collection, *Nervous Arcs* published in 1995, contained a number of poems and sequences redacted from archival materials. Then, I thought I was writing about other people's lives, but of course I was writing about myself. When I look over the subjects of that first book—Emily Dickinson, Frida Kahlo, Ahab, Frankenstein—I'm struck by the clear connection between me and them, and my writing is certainly not as subjective as I then thought.

Over time I've come to accept that my work can never be totally objective and that I exist in each and every poem despite its subject matter. I've even begun to enjoy this concept. I can adopt other personas as a foil for my own, write about everything I feel I either can't or don't want to express, with that enormous eye of public judgement comfortably and conveniently trained on someone else.

With this realisation in mind, I approached my second collection, *Botany Bay Document*, which is subtitled, *A Poetic History of the Women of Botany Bay*. For six months, I devoured pertinent letters, diaries, maps, ship logs and so on, foraging for traces of the women who had come to Australia either as convicts or by their own free will during the first 25 years of white settlement. I also visited Sydney's Hyde Park Barracks. The ground-level floorboards had been recently lifted and on display was a huge assortment of clay pipes. There were over 5,000 pipes—everybody smoked, even children—as well as cutlery, keys and other items that had fallen or been pushed through the floor's cracks. I was particularly taken by the collection of rag tampons. I was acutely aware that this was a piece of women's history I was very fortunate to view.

With my next collection, *The Hanging of Jean Lee*, I wanted to concentrate on one woman alone. I searched a long time to find the right subject for my writing. Jean Lee was one of only five women ever hanged in this country and the only one to be executed in the twentieth century. My intellect told me, 'this is a story that must be told', while my imagination told me, 'this woman is like me in so many ways'. That is when the pot starts melting and poetry sometimes happens. When you feel your own core blink with recognition and begin to write.

Research for this collection involved the usual intensive survey of archival documents, as well as more personal experiences like visiting H Division in Pentridge, being locked in the cell where Jean was kept in solitary confinement and running my hands over the rope grooves in the hanging beam. I wanted to tell her story, but I also wanted to express my own aloneness, my own downfall if you like, my story. While I've never been a prostitute or an accomplice to murder like Jean, I have experienced my own mistakes and misunderstandings, my own solitary confinement, and I found many instances where I felt Jean's presence as I wrote.

Following *The Hanging of Jean Lee*, I left documentary poetry alone for a few years in order to focus on my other preoccupation, the mathematics of poetic form. It wasn't until 2013 that I returned to the genre with *The Book of Ethel.* This collection comprises micro portraits of my own maternal great-grandmother who emigrated from St Just in Cornwall to Australia in 1872 at the age of 15. She married a Methodist minister and they settled first in a one-room tin shack outside Mildura. She lived until 1949, moving house frequently and raising six children along the way.

The poetry here is formal and concise, employing a strict external and internal rhyme scheme. Each poem comprises a seven-line stanza and each line contains seven syllables. With a plethora of family documents and regalia at hand along with the privilege of a writer's residency in Cornwall which allowed me that holy grail, a witness of place, I sought to accord Ethel her own voice while exploring the tensions between high poetic artifice and the smaller moments of an ordinary life. A number of Cornish words found their way into the poems and I provided a glossary at the back of the book.

Again, it was several years and a few further books before I came back to documentary poetry with a collection called *Warlines.* In 2017, I received a fellowship from the State Library of Victoria. My project there was the redaction into poetry of letters written home by Victorian soldiers during the First World War. As is the way with all documentary work, much pre-poetry footwork was required: the reading of hundreds of letters, the selection process, the choice of which poetic structures to employ, copyright issues, etc.

The poems are formatted as letter blocks, justified on both right and left sides, however many closed forms are contained within these blocks from the pantoum, villanelle and sestina to the palindrome, sonnet and hymn. A further constraint I set myself was that I employed none of my own words, thus restricting the poems to a kind of literary mosaic of each soldier's individual correspondence. Sometimes this meant conflating many letters into one poem, at other times a soldier may have penned only a couple of letters or postcards home.

The publication of my latest collection, *Frank*, represents a perfect circle. Much of the work was created during my Creative Arts Fellowship for Australian

Writing at the National Library of Australia, inspired by the material in their collection, and this book is now being published by the National Library's imprint. The single-word title functions both as name and descriptor: my subject, Frank Hurley, was a very frank writer.

Frank Hurley was an Australian adventurer and photographer who accompanied both Mawson and Shackleton on separate expeditions to Antarctica in the early twentieth century at the end of the heroic age of exploration. His photos are the first to record the incredible snowscapes and wildlife of the region, as well as capturing the work and lives of his crew and comrades. Most people will have encountered, at some point, these spectacular black and white photographs of blizzards, an ice wall or ice cliff off Adélie Land, an ice cave showing the refraction of light into the space, a meteorologist with his Burberry all iced in around his face, Royal Penguins on Macquarie Island. Hurley was taking these pictures in extreme conditions. As Mawson later wrote in *Home of the Blizzard*, this was 'an accursed country … On the fringe of an unspanned continent … we dwelt where the chill breath of a vast, Polar wilderness, quickening to the rushing might of eternal blizzards, surged to the northern seas'.

Hurley, like many of his fellow expeditioners, was an avid diarist. It is these writings that I've deciphered, imbibed and transmogrified into the realm of poetry here. The poetry is divided into three sections, each section derived from a different diary. First, the sledging diary detailing Sir Douglas Mawson's Australasian Antarctic Division expedition in 1912–1913; second, the imperial transantarctic Shackleton expedition diary of 1914–1916; and third, the touring diary of the Shackleton picture show called 'In the Grip of the Polar Pack Ice', which screened across Sydney, Melbourne, Adelaide and Brisbane during 1919 and 1920. As with *Warlines*, these poems contain none of my own words. What I'm doing is taking phrases, fragments and images and collocating them under the pressure of poetic form in order to create something new.

I was drawn to this material for a number of reasons, not least the concept of entering a place totally new, totally alien and almost totally white. This in itself triggered a heavy and elaborate response in me, which I felt impelled to further interrogate. This was my chance to cross over into an expanse of seeming endlessness and silence. Then there were the key notions of survival, endurance, discovery, spectacle and awe. These expeditions to the far south seemed to reverberate not only at the manifest and obvious historical level but also at a deeply human one.

Hurley's pictures and writings transport us swiftly to the hub of what it means to live. Hardship and perseverance, tolerance and cooperation, friendship and sustenance, vision, honest toil and the hope of some sense of reward at the eventual end of that toil. Also, of course, an encounter with the natural world and its wildlife in a hitherto unmapped and unexplored, that is to say unknown, context. The sad fact that the Antarctic was altering and diminishing beneath the barrage of global warming as I wrote provided yet another layer of heat to the task.

I had already completed the first Mawson section before I applied for a fellowship at the National Library of Australia. Here, the poems are formatted as run-on justified blocks with their relevant journal dates as titles. Each poem represents a sort of tapestry of that particular original diary entry, complete with misspellings, crossings out and grammatical peccadilloes. Each poem is compressed and figured according to the musical precepts of poetry, in particular in this case rhythm and internal rhyme. One poem in this section, 'November 16, 1912', is a pantoum, which is a class of chained verse involving a specific pattern of line repetition. As with all the *Frank* poems, the schema is sparse, and dashes and lacunae, or spaces, are employed in place of punctuation.

The second Shackleton section is more complex than the first Mawson section, as Hurley's diary of this expedition is much longer, requiring more aggressive, more meticulous organisational techniques. I've coded the primary source material according to six principal and recurring motifs; a day, a night, a month, a vista, a note and a snap. Examples of note poems include a note about dogs, a note about hunting and a note about ice. These poems involved pecking like a magpie through the huge two-volume diary for suitable fragments. The vista poems explore subjects such as a vista of Elephant Island, a vista of pressure, a vista of Sir E (Ernest Shackleton).

The tour diary that inspired the third section exists in handwritten form only. His writing is often in pencil and barely legible. I spent a fortnight in the National Library's Special Collections Reading Room transcribing this material and these two weeks proved critical to me as a poet. Climate, haste, leisure, stress, excitement, fatigue—it's all there in Hurley's handwriting, even alcohol. The writer's mood is far more readily detected than in its typescript counterpart. As a result, I found poems arriving in the very act of transcription, which is always magic.

This final section is the most complicated of the three. I utilised fragments and phrases from the tour diary and interspersed these with metaphorically germane fragments from the diary concerning the Shackleton expedition itself. These long poems have titles that relate both to the world of theatrical film and to the Antarctic: scenery, season, soliloquy, refreshments, interlude, accompaniment, finale.

It can be arduous and unpredictable work using recorded history as a springboard for one's own imagination. Researching the past and recycling it involves the melding of one's present self and all those past selves, however they're perceived. Maybe it's all we can do as poets, as writers, to create a personal kind of order out of the overwhelming rush of information we're presented with during our time on this earth. We're each unique beings but we are also the product to a large extent of what has gone on before.

As Rilke points out, we always have our own childhoods, our individual pasts, as an enormous source of material for poetry. Yet, Rilke lived in a different culture and a different time. Perhaps the present state of the environment, of the world and of its inhabitants lends a greater urgency to the enterprise of rewriting history as an act of the imagination. As COVID continues its march across the world, along with countless other marches just as urgent, just as tragic, what have we learned about the role of history in our creative lives?

Dr Jordie Albiston (30 September 1961–1 March 2022)

This is an abridged transcript of the speech Jordie gave at the National Library of Australia on 18 March 2021 as part of her Creative Arts Fellowship for Australian Writing. You can view the full speech online at:

nla.gov.au/stories/video/fellowship-presentation-frank-hurley-antarctica.

Dr Jordie Albiston passed away suddenly during the production of *Frank*. The National Library of Australia mourns her loss.

acknowledgements

Grateful acknowledgement is due to the National Library of Australia for awarding the 2021 Creative Arts Fellowship for Australian Writing in support of the research and writing of *Frank*. This work is based on diaries forming part of 'The Papers of Frank Hurley 1912–1962', MS883 (Series 1, Items 2–4 and Item 6), held at the National Library of Australia.

Warm thanks are also extended to Julie Byrnes—granddaughter of Frank Hurley—for her kind endorsement of this project.

Excerpts from several poems appear in Professor Jessica Wilkinson's essay 'The Precise Punctuation of Your Breath: Jordie Albiston's Oeuvre', *Sydney Review of Books*, Oct. 2022.

images:

Cover Frank Hurley, *A Turreted Berg*, Australasian Antarctic Expedition, c.1913, nla. cat-vn1550641

Endpapers Frank Hurley, *Panoramic View of the Discovery Passing through Icepacks*, c.1929, nla.cat-vn4973532; Frank Hurley, *Panoramic View of the Discovery with Crew on Board*, c.1929, nla.cat-vn4973529

10 Frank Hurley, *Self Portrait*, c.1911, National Portrait Gallery 2005.103

12–13 Frank Hurley, *Steaming through Light Pack-ice*, Australasian Antarctic Expedition, between 1911 and 1914, nla.cat-vn3255263

26 *Frank Hurley in Front of the Hut on Elephant Island, Imperial Trans Antarctic Expedition*, between 1914 and 1917, Alamy Image A62F27

28–29 Frank Hurley, *As Time Wore on It Became More and More Evident That the Ship Was Doomed*, Shackleton Expedition, 1915, nla.cat-vn92302

130 Walter Burke, *Wally Shiers, Frank Hurley, Keith Smith and Jim Bennett with the Vickers Vimy*, 1920, State Library NSW DG ON 2/2

132–133 Frank Hurley, *Composite Image Used on Hurley's Picture Show Tour; View of Interior of Hut on Elephant Island*, Shackleton Expedition, 1916, nla.cat-vn2011980

148–149 *Frank Hurley Filming from the Tip of the Discovery's Jib-boom*, c.1930, nla.cat-vn781937

151 *Portrait of Jordie Albiston*, 2020, courtesy Andy Szikla